Exploring Outdoor Play in the Early Years

Exploring Outdoor Play in the Early Years

Edited by
Trisha Maynard and Jane Waters

Mc
Graw
Hill
Education Open University Press

Open University Press
McGraw-Hill Education
McGraw-Hill House
Shoppenhangers Road
Maidenhead
Berkshire
England
SL6 2QL

email: enquiries@openup.co.uk
world wide web: www.openup.co.uk

and Two Penn Plaza, New York, NY 10121-2289, USA

First published 2014

Copyright © Trisha Maynard and Jane Waters, 2014

A catalogue record of this book is available from the British Library

ISBN-13: 978-0-335-26338-7
ISBN-10: 0-335-26338-0
eISBN: 978-0-335-26339-4

Library of Congress Cataloging-in-Publication Data
CIP data applied for

Typeset by Aptara Inc., India

Praise for this book

"This is a thought provoking book that draws on research to encourage the reader to reflect on the essence of outdoor play in early childhood. Recognising that within our society assumptions are made about outdoors and about childhood, this book challenges the reader to reflect on outdoor provision from a number of perspectives. The outdoor environment matters to young children. This book not only makes the case for outdoor play, it considers what that actually looks like in the UK and internationally, and asks us to reflect on the implications for our own working practices. Maynard and Waters set out to provoke critical reflection and inspire practitioners; they have certainly achieved their aim and this book is a welcome addition to the debate about outdoors in the early years."

Gail Ryder Richardson, Early Years Consultant and Trainer, Outdoor Matters!

Praise for this book

Contents

Contributors

Valerie Huggins

Valerie is an experienced lecturer in early childhood studies at Plymouth University, with a lead role in early years teacher education and professional studies. Before taking up her current post, she spent many years working as an early years teacher and consultant and some time with VSO training teacher educators in Ethiopia. Her research interests centre on different approaches to effective early years education, both in the UK and in Majority World contexts, including the use of the outdoor environment. Valerie is studying for a Doctorate in Education with a focus on interculturality.

Sara Knight

Sara has recently retired from her post as a principal lecturer at Anglia Ruskin University to concentrate on her work on early years experiential outdoor learning. She is a trained Forest School practitioner and a founder member of the Forest School Association in the UK. Her books cover Forest School with all ages in the UK and outdoor learning with younger children across the world. Sara worked in schools and nurseries in the UK before embarking on an academic career, and continues both to write and to get outside into wilder spaces with young children.

Dr Helen Little

Helen is a lecturer at the Institute of Early Childhood, Macquarie University, Australia where she teaches on undergraduate and postgraduate units in child development. She is a trained early childhood teacher and previously taught in preschools and primary schools in Sydney. She has been investigating children's risk-taking since 2007 and her doctoral thesis examined the influence of individual, social and environmental factors on children's engagement in risk-taking behaviour in outdoor play. Her current focus relates to how the space and physical features available in the outdoor environment impact on children's experiences of risk-taking in play.

Professor Trisha Maynard

Trisha is Professor of Early Childhood Spaces and Director of the Research Centre for Children, Families and Communities at Canterbury Christ Church University. Trisha taught in an infant school before being appointed as tutor on the Primary PGCE at Swansea University in 1991. Trisha remained at Swansea for 19 years; from 2007 as Professor of Early Childhood Studies. Trisha's most recent research – much of which has been undertaken in collaboration with

Jane Waters – has focused on the Foundation Phase for Wales, the philosophy of the preschools of Reggio Emilia, and outdoor play and learning.

Dr Ellen Beate Hansen Sandseter

Ellen is an associate professor (PhD) in the Department of Physical Education at Queen Maud University College of Early Childhood Education (DMMH) in Trondheim, Norway. Her primary research focus is on children's physical play, outdoor play and risky/thrilling play among children in Early Childhood Education and Care (ECEC) institutions. She has cooperated with early childhood researchers from both England and Australia to study cultural differences in provision of outdoor – and risky – play in ECEC settings. Recently she has been involved in a study of Norwegian children's experiences of participation and wellbeing in Norwegian ECEC institutions as well as project mapping all child accidents and injuries in Norwegian ECEC institutions.

Dr Alison Stephenson

Alison is now an honorary research associate with Victoria University Wellington, after more than 20 years teaching in the university's early childhood teacher education programmes. Her exploration of young children's outdoor activities in an early childhood education centre for her Master's thesis, and her further research, writing and teaching in this area, are a reflection of her own lifestyle and interests.

Helen Tovey

Helen is Principal Lecturer in Early Childhood Studies at University of Roehampton, London where she teaches on BA and MA and professional development courses. Her main research interests are outdoor play and young children's risk-taking outdoors. Helen is a Froebel trained teacher and a former nursery school headteacher. She is author of numerous texts including *Playing Outdoors: Spaces and Places, Risk and Challenge* (Open University Press) and *Bringing the Froebel Approach to your Early Years Practice* (Routledge).

Sue Waite

Sue is Associate Professor (Reader) in the Plymouth Institute of Education. Her research into outdoor learning includes studies of Forest School, decline of provision of outdoor learning in schools and issues of transition, health and wellbeing outcomes from woodland activities, place-based learning and social and economic aspirations and realities for rural young people. She currently leads the Natural Connections Demonstration Project funded by Natural England, DEFRA and English Heritage and convenes Plymouth University outdoor and experiential learning research network. Sue sits on the editorial board of *Education 3–13, Pastoral Care in Education* and the *Journal of Experiential Education.*

Dr Jane Waters

Jane is Director of Primary Programmes in the South West Wales Centre of Teacher Education based at the University of Wales Trinity Saint David: Swansea and Carmarthen. Jane worked in mainstream schools teaching primary age children before moving to the HE sector to contribute to initial teacher education and then to lead an early childhood studies undergraduate programme. She recently completed her PhD, which focused on child-initiated interaction between early years children and their teachers in the outdoors, and the associated opportunities for sustained and shared thinking. Jane's current research activity is related to educative interaction in the early years and the contribution of different spaces to such interaction.

Jan White

Jan works nationally and internationally to advocate and support high quality outdoor provision for services for children from birth to 7. With 28 years' experience of working in education, she is currently an Early Education founding associate, adviser for several landscape and equipment companies and mentor to Sandfield Natural Play Centre. She teaches on the Masters programme at CREC (Birmingham City University). She is author of a number of texts including *Playing and Learning Outdoors: Making Provision for High Quality Experiences in the Outdoor Environment with children 3–7* (Routledge) and collaborated with Siren Films to make the award-winning training DVDs *Babies Outdoors, Toddlers Outdoors* and *Two Year Olds Outdoors*.

Karen Wickett

Karen is a lecturer in early childhood studies at Plymouth University. She teaches on the BEd and BA Early Childhood Studies degrees. Originally she qualified as an NNEB and later trained as a teacher. Between 2003 and 2012 she worked in a Sure Start Local Programme/children's centre. During this period she supported many practitioners to develop their understanding of teaching and learning in the outdoors. Currently she is undertaking her EdD at Plymouth University. She is researching parents', teachers' and EY practitioners' experiences of supporting children's transition to school and understanding of school readiness.

Helen Woolley

Helen is a Chartered Landscape Architect and Reader in Landscape Architecture and Society at The University of Sheffield. Her research interests relate to children's use of a range of domestic, neighbourhood and civic outdoor environments including green spaces in housing areas, school playgrounds, children's centres, public parks, playgrounds and city centre outdoor spaces. Helen is increasingly interested in how these outdoor environments are controlled by adults, both individuals and mechanisms within society. Helen's research has also explored issues around urban green spaces with much of this work being undertaken for government and national organizations. Helen was a CABE Ssace enabler between 2003 and 2011. This range of research informs her knowledge exchange activities with partners outside the university and her teaching with undergraduate, postgraduate and research students.

Dr Shirley Wyver

Shirley is a senior lecturer in child development at the Institute of Early Childhood, Macquarie University, Australia. Her research interests are in early play and cognitive/social development. Her major research in this area is conducted with a multidisciplinary team known as the Sydney Playground Project. She also conducts research in the area of blindness/low vision and development.

Introduction: outdoor play in early years settings

Jane Waters and Trisha Maynard

Introduction

Within much of the western world, there has been evidence since the early 1990s of an increasing concern that children need to be protected – particularly, though not exclusively, from the dangers lurking outdoors. Frank Furedi (2008) argues that such a concern has resulted in 'paranoid parenting' while Thomas and Hocking (2003) refer to the 'colonisation' of children's lives by adults – in an attempt to keep children safe and occupied they are escorted to and from numerous organized recreational activities and spend time, often alone in their bedrooms, watching television or playing computer games. Such contained, constrained and sedentary lifestyles have also been associated with concerns about children's physical health and mental wellbeing (e.g. Palmer 2007), their loss of affinity with nature (e.g. Louv 2010, 2013), and even the loss of childhood itself (e.g. Bailey 2011). It is unsurprising perhaps that a recent campaign in the UK by the makers of a washing powder ('Dirt is Good') suggested that before the age of 10 children should, for example, roll down a grassy bank; make a mud pie; collect frogspawn; make perfume from flower petals; climb a tree; build a den . . . simple, innocent fun. And it may also be unsurprising that such images call out to our hearts and imaginations; they appear to resonate with deeply embedded ideas within many western cultures about a 'golden age' of childhood innocence, even if such images do not entirely represent individual childhoods either past or present.

In relation to young children, it may not be by coincidence, then, that as such concerns have become increasingly visible within the media, and as the amount of outdoor play afforded to early years children in educational settings has declined (Bilton 2002), UK policy makers have articulated their intention to raise the status of outdoor play within early years curricula.

It is important to note here that within this volume we do not intend to focus specifically on the nature or value of 'play': this has been considered in depth elsewhere (e.g. Moyles 2010; Wood 2013). Rather, as we shall see, this text seeks to unpick and critically respond to some of the most significant concerns and issues relating to the provision of outdoor experiences for young children from birth to 8 years – primarily in the UK but also within Scandinavia, New Zealand and Australia. These include: space, activity, freedom, safety and risk. In considering these issues the authors refer to the impact of broader circulating 'discourses' and related constructs and practices. In doing so, we attempt to build on the foundations set by the classic texts on outdoor play and learning to confront the contemporary challenges faced by current early years practitioners. And within the UK in particular, given the demands of addressing the requirements of a statutory curriculum that does not foreground children's outdoor play or which retains subject-related outcomes, the challenges for early years practitioners may be significant.

Considering the sociocultural context

As we have indicated above, it is important to set outdoor play within the broader context of circulating concerns. In order to do this, it is helpful to consider sociocultural theory as it applies to young children's development and learning.

Socio cultural or socio cultural historical theory (see, for example, Anning et al. 2009) is generally taken to represent a range of theories that include Vygotskian and post-Vygotskian (e.g. socio-constructivist) perspectives as well as aspects of post-modern/post-structuralist theory. Such theories propose that children's development and learning are embedded within particular social, cultural and historical contexts; development and learning take place as a result of the child's participation in the activities of his or her cultural community.

In addition, post-structuralist ideas relating to 'discourse' are also relevant here. Within post structuralist theory, as we have noted elsewhere (Maynard 2007; Maynard et al. 2013b), society is seen as divided into many social and cultural fields (e.g. politics, education), each field speaking to itself and of itself through 'discourses': particular and shared languages, meanings and practices (Danaher et al. 2000). At any one time, certain discourses are officially sanctioned and become dominant within the field. These discourses form 'regimes of truth' that govern what are held to be 'normal and desirable ways to think, act and feel' (MacNaughton 2005: 32). However, it is maintained, we can resist the practices of power and normalization (Danaher et al. 2000); we can destabilize officially sanctioned truths (MacNaughton 2005). That is, through making visible, deconstructing, problematizing and questioning dominant discourses and the constructions and practices they produce, it is possible to create spaces 'in which alternative discourses and constructions can be produced' (Dahlberg et al. 1999: 34).

Considering early years practice through a sociocultural historical lens helps us to make visible some of the embedded assumptions and unarticulated understandings that underpin the unspoken 'truths' – particular ways of thinking and being – that are dominant within particular contexts. As noted above, one commonly accepted 'truth' in recent times has been the construction of the child as vulnerable and weak. Early years practitioners accepting this 'truth' are likely to see as a priority the need to protect young children from harm. Such a priority may mean that risk-taking is limited and children are not expected to experience wet or cold weather conditions. A further 'truth' may be the acceptance of the Romantic construction of the innocent child who is naturally 'at home' in a green space (e.g. see Taylor 2013), a 'truth' that is embedded within the early years tradition. This 'truth', which may sit uneasily against the need to protect the child, may support the carefree exploration of natural spaces by young children although practitioners may also be shocked and dismayed when children try to trap or destructively explore the mini-beasts encountered with the space!

As we shall see, an important aim of this text, then, is to encourage readers to uncover and question these accepted 'truths'.

Working in different sociocultural contexts

It is important to note that the chapter authors in this text are working in different sociocultural historical contexts that prioritize – officially sanction – particular and often different discourses. For example, the chapter on outdoor play in Scandinavia indicates a cultural construct of the child as being competent and capable and thus given considerable freedom outdoors; as noted above, such a view is not officially accepted as a 'given' across much of the western world at the present time. At the same time, however, Sandseter (Chapter 8) notes a move towards more outcomes-focused learning in Scandinavia: a concern shared by many other authors.

Conflicting discourses and constructs are likely to present practitioners with real challenges. This may particularly be the case when practitioners are required to work within a detailed and content-focused curriculum. How to manage the requirement to keep children 'safe' while encouraging appropriate and developmentally beneficial risk-taking is one example; another is how to provide children with opportunities to lead their learning outdoors while simultaneously ensuring that variously prescribed curricular objectives are met.

What constitutes a 'cultural context' can, of course, be interpreted in different ways – for example, Waters (Chapter 7) refers to the culture of particular spaces. And it would certainly be mistaken to assume that practitioners across the UK are working within identical policy contexts; there are important differences that are evident within the relevant documentation. While many UK-based texts position themselves within the context of English policy, we feel it is important, also, to 'set the scene' for this volume by providing an overview of outdoor play within the policy documents of the four legislative areas of the UK, namely: Scotland, Wales, Northern Ireland and England.

The UK policy context

While similar themes are addressed within these policy documents there are significant differences in the stated rationale for, or purposes of, children's playful
and educational experiences outside. In Scotland and Wales, for example, there
is an explicit and clearly stated government commitment to children's engagement in playful learning outdoors throughout the early years. There is also an
explicit expectation that children experience elements of risk in their play in
these countries. Such a commitment is not apparent in the policy documents
for Northern Ireland and England and therefore will provide a different – and
powerful – policy context for the work of early years practitioners.

Scotland: Curriculum for Excellence

The Curriculum for Excellence in Scotland is applicable to learners from 3–18
years of age in Scotland. It includes the totality of experiences which are planned
for children and young people through their education, wherever they are
being educated (Education Scotland 2013). It aims to develop four capacities,
helping children to become: successful learners; confident individuals; responsible citizens; and effective contributors. Curriculum areas and subjects are
the 'organizers' for setting out the experiences and outcomes for learners and
each area contributes to the four capacities. Learning takes place within and
across curriculum areas and is meant to include and build on learning that
takes place beyond the education setting, in the community and family for
example. The Scottish Government has explicitly set out a commitment to outdoor learning by publishing a school curriculum for learning in the outdoors.
The guidance document 'makes it clear that the outdoor environment offers
motivating, exciting, different, relevant and easily accessible activities from
pre-school years through to college' (Learning and Teaching Scotland 2010: 3).

The rationale for outdoor learning in Scotland is articulated at the level
of strategic aims and individual personal development. Strategically, outdoor
learning is linked to life-long learning, improved health outcomes, stronger
communities, sustainable futures and improved outcomes for individuals in
the long term. The Scottish Government asserts a need for children and young
people to 'have opportunities to develop skills to assess and manage risk when
making decisions' (Learning and Teaching Scotland 2010: 5) and associates this
with outdoor learning opportunities.

At the level of individual development outdoor provision is linked to
'the wellbeing of [Scotland's] children and young people' and to them becoming 'resilient, responsible citizens and successful lifelong learners, who value
[Scotland's] landscape and culture and contribute effectively to [Scotland's]
local and global society' (Learning and Teaching Scotland 2010: 7). Outdoor learning is seen as resonating with the core values of Curriculum for
Excellence: 'Challenge, enjoyment, relevance, depth, development of the whole

person and an adventurous approach to learning are at the core of outdoor pedagogy. The outdoor environment encourages staff and students to see each other in a different light, building positive relationships and improving self-awareness and understanding of others' (p. 7).

The vision for outdoor provision is that it is relevant to the curriculum, involves regular outdoor experiences which are embedded in the life of the setting and that learning experiences are progressive and creative. That the Scottish Government has set out, clearly and explicitly, the requirement to include significant outdoor provision in children's educational life indicates a national mandate within which all settings operate. Arguably the clear rationale and explicit directive supports practitioners in working within their local communities to provide meaningful and challenging outdoor play and provision from the early years and beyond.

There is a similar governmental commitment to outdoor learning within the Welsh Government, though the rationale for this is arguably less clearly articulated.

Wales: Foundation Phase Framework

The Foundation Phase Framework for Children's Learning aged 3–7 in Wales (DCELLS 2008) is described as being based on 'the principle that early years' provision should offer a sound foundation for future learning through a developmentally appropriate curriculum' and placing 'great emphasis on children learning by doing' (Welsh Government 2012: 1). In the Foundation Phase 'young children will be given more opportunities to gain first hand experiences through play and active involvement rather than by completing exercises in books' (p. 1). The emphasis of provision is based on experiential learning, active involvement and children understanding how things work and solving problems.

The Foundation Phase curriculum is organized under seven areas of learning and there are content-specific learning outcomes at the age of 7 as well as an expectation that children will have reached a specific level of skill in literacy and numeracy by this age (Welsh Government 2013). Tensions exist between the content-based outcomes and process-based expectation of provision within the Foundation Phase documentation (Maynard et al. 2013a); however, the Welsh Government makes an explicit commitment to the provision of meaningful outdoor experiences for all children in the Foundation Phase.

The Foundation Phase outdoor learning handbook states that 'the Foundation Phase and the outdoors are inseparable' (DCELLS 2009: 2). The rationale for this commitment is based on the assertion that the outdoors is the 'ideal environment for experiential learning, because it offers unique opportunities to be creative, to move around, to be noisy and to take risks' (DCELLS 2009: 2). Being outdoors is seen to enhance all aspects of children's development and support children's ability to learn and to retain their learning. Specific benefits are seen to relate to health and fitness, experience of the natural world, the opportunities provided for authentic problem solving and first-hand experience of conservation and sustainability.

The Welsh Government sets out an explicit approach to children's risk-taking, expecting settings to 'enable children to take appropriate risks' (DCELLS 2009: 4) because '[e]xposure to acceptable risk is a fundamental part of outdoor learning and such exposure can help avoid children seeking the thrill of risk in more dangerous, unsupervised situations' (p. 4). The Welsh Government documentation and rationale for outdoor learning provides a similar mandate for early years practitioners in Wales to that provided in Scotland, actively supporting settings in their work to develop and maintain effective outdoor provision.

Northern Ireland: Foundation Stage

In Northern Ireland children aged 3–5 follow the Foundation Stage curriculum (NIC 2006). The aim of the Foundation Stage is to 'empower young people to develop their potential and make informed and responsible choices and decisions throughout their lives' (p. 3). Young children are seen as learning best when learning is 'interactive, practical and enjoyable for both children and teachers' (NIC 2006: 4); when they are engaged in varied and changing environments in which they can make choices and initiate experiences within well-established positive relationships. The curriculum is organized under seven areas of learning with specific content-related outcomes at the age of 5. The Foundation Stage documentation makes little reference to the outdoor environment other than to state an expectation that the indoor and outdoor environment should be well presented and creatively resourced.

The Early Years Interboard Panel (EYIP) produced a guidance document when the Foundation Stage was in its proposal stage in 2005. This document is given as a link on the Foundation Stage website pages (NIC 2013) and so is taken as government-endorsed guidance for outdoor provision. This document adopts Helen Bilton's guiding principles for outdoor play in the early years (e.g. Bilton 2002) as its underpinning rationale and states the purpose of outdoor play is to support children's physical, social and emotional development and wellbeing. The document sets out ideas for provision of play spaces under the seven areas of learning. No claims are made at governmental level or in the guidance document for any further rationale for young children's access to the outdoors. The mandate, then, for practitioners in Northern Ireland extends to curriculum-related provision of varied play environments. Arguably, this is considerably more limited than the mandate provided to those working in Scotland and Wales.

England: Early Years Foundation Stage

In England, the Early Years Foundation Stage (EYFS, DfE 2012) is the statutory framework document for all those providing care and education for children aged from birth to 5 years. The framework is explicit in its aim to ensure children's 'school readiness' at the age of 5:

> Every child deserves the best possible start in life and the support that
> enables them to fulfill their potential . . . [the EYFS] sets the standards
> that all early years providers must meet to ensure that children learn
> and develop well and are kept healthy and safe. It promotes teaching
> and learning to ensure children's 'school readiness' and gives children
> the broad range of knowledge and skills that provide the right founda-
> tion for good future progress through school and life.
>
> (DfE 2012: 2)

The EYFS specifies required curriculum content, assessment and reporting
measures and expected outcomes for children. The pedagogical approach in
EYFS settings is shaped by four guiding principles, namely: every child is a
unique, capable child; children learn to be strong and independent through positive relationships; children learn and develop well in enabling environments;
and children develop and learn in different ways and at different rates.

The curriculum is organized into three *prime* areas of learning and four
specific areas. The prime areas are: communication and language; physical
development; and personal, social and emotional development. The specific
areas, through which the three prime areas are strengthened and applied,
are: literacy; mathematics; understanding the world; and expressive arts and
design. There is minimal reference to learning or playing outdoors other than
the requirement for providers to 'provide access to an outdoor play area or, if
that is not possible, ensure that outdoor activities are planned and taken on a
daily basis' (DfE 2012: 24) and to 'ensure that their premises, including outdoor
spaces, are fit for purpose' (DfE 2012: 23), safe, secure and clean. Clearly practitioners are able to interpret the requirement to provide 'enabling environments',
outdoors and indoors, as they wish. The DfE website does not provide any links
to related documents pertaining to learning outside and it is interesting to note
that the publication *Learning Outside the Classroom Manifesto* (DfES 2006),
which set out a clear and directive mandate for practitioners to move beyond
the school grounds when planning educational provision, has been archived on
the Department for Education website and is not to be considered to 'reflect
current policy or guidance' (DfE 2013).

While recognizing the gulf that may exist between policy and practice, it
appears that it is in England then, of all the UK legislative regions, that the government mandate for early years children to play/learn outdoors is the weakest.
Whether the status of outdoor play in any future documentation is strengthened
or further eroded remains to be seen.

The central aim and structure of this text

As we indicated above, then, given the power of statutory curricula (and to
a greater or lesser extent, the lack of early years practitioners' power and

autonomy) we would argue that the dominant, and sometimes conflicting, discourses and associated constructs and practices that may be hidden within policy documents, as well as those more broadly circulating within particular sociocultural historical contexts, or even within the early years 'tradition', should be made visible and questioned. This is likely to include questioning the underpinning construct of the child (as innocent and in need of protection) as well as challenging any uncritical adoption of any natural and *inherently* beneficial association between young children and the outdoors. When problematized in this way, the question 'what constitutes a "good" outdoor environment?' takes on a new meaning: it leads to the question *'good for what?'* A central aim of this book, then, is to challenge readers to recognize, question, and, where deemed appropriate, attempt to resist dominant discourses and their related constructs and practices.

The book specifically addresses three issues:

- what constitutes 'good' outdoor provision for young children and babies;
- how we respect and respond to the young child in outdoor provision; and
- how we support risky play within the bounds of a statutory curriculum or a restrictive regulatory regime.

Underpinning a consideration of these issues is an acknowledgement of play as the primary (though not the sole) means through which young children learn. In addition, our authors all argue that the child is, and should be recognized as, competent and strong; in different ways they each stress the need to attend to the child's voice in a genuine manner within practice.

The text is structured in three sections. Section 1 begins by exploring why outdoor play is considered important in relation to young children's care and education today; how outdoor play supports the developing child; and what is seen as a 'good' outdoor environment according to children, adults and those working in the field.

Helen Tovey's chapter focuses on the rich tradition of ideas concerning the value of the outdoors for young children's play and learning. Helen argues that thinking about the 'early years tradition' is not about looking back and trying to preserve outdated theories or practices, but is about deepening our understanding of the roots of current ideas and practices in ways which can enrich, sharpen and sometimes challenge our ideas and practices today and help shape those of the future. Froebel's notion of the nursery 'garden' and the principles which underpinned his ideas of the importance of direct experience of nature outdoors are critically considered alongside the distinctive contributions of Margaret McMillan, Susan Isaacs and Marjorie Allen. The notion of adventurous play outdoors as part of the early years tradition is discussed in relation to current ideas and practices concerning risk and safety; we are challenged to reconsider the widespread view that use of wild and woodland spaces in the UK are a recent development.

Jan White and Helen Woolley explore emerging 'characteristics' of space, place, provision and organization that make a significant contribution to the experience of the children who 'inhabit' a space. In this chapter the authors draw from literature in several fields, such as early childhood development, early years education, landscape architecture, playwork, children's geographies, environmental psychology, evolutionary biology and body and movement studies. This chapter challenges us to reconsider what we mean by 'good' provision of outdoor experiences in ways that are fundamental to the experience of the child. Drawing on an ecological approach, where the child and the environment are in 'dialogue' through a feedback cycle, and the perspectives of children, educators and landscape professionals, the authors explore how design, provision and operation of outdoor play and learning environments can maximize young children's opportunities.

Jan White then provides a chapter focusing on outdoor provision for the very youngest children from birth to 2. She provides a contemporary rationale and theoretical basis to support decision-making about such provision and challenges us to reconsider approaches that may be underpinned by notions of vulnerability and a discourse of protection for this age group.

Section 2 focuses on issues that impact upon outdoor play provision in the UK. Building on the overview of different UK early years curricula provided in this introduction, the text identifies a number of key issues for practice: supporting child-initiated learning; providing for and managing risky play; working with Forest Schools; and how practitioners can get the most out of their outdoor spaces and learn about how children perceive their outdoor environments.

Set within a consideration of child-centred and subject-centred approaches, Trisha Maynard's chapter explores what is meant by child-initiated activity and its significance for young children. Drawing on the findings of a number of research projects based in Wales, Trisha identifies the specific challenges faced by early years teachers when attempting to support child-initiated activity, arguing that the outdoor environment provides a particularly appropriate and supportive context, both for children and their teachers.

In the second chapter in this section, Sue Waite, Valerie Huggins and Karen Wickett provide a definition of what constitutes 'risky play' and its relationship to challenge in learning, and suggest why it is valuable to include such opportunities in early years practice. The authors examine temporally and culturally situated conceptualizations of childhood to examine how underlying views of the child shape the provision that adults are willing to provide for young children. In their critically considered stance they also reinforce the notion that evangelism has little place in the establishment of a clearly articulated and rational approach to the provision of appropriately risky experiences in children's encounters with the environment.

Sara Knight then explores the ethos, principles and practice of Forest School, in order to articulate the ways in which this particular experience in the UK differs from other outdoor provision. The author places Forest School in its cultural and historical context and considers the notion that wilder spaces are important to children's sense of place, to their engagement with their environment, and to their confidence as agents in control of their own space. The author reminds us of the need for continued research to capture the lived experiences, and longer-term outcomes, of Forest School in order to fully understand the powerful potential that the Forest School experience appears to offer.

The final chapter in this section is provided by Jane Waters who considers questions concerning the evaluation and development of children's activity in outdoor spaces. She proposes a model for evaluating activity in outdoor space with a view to identifying what practitioners can change in order to ensure that young children are getting the most from their outdoor experiences. The model is based on the concept of affordance, which is explained and used to demonstrate aspects that influence and impact upon children's activity when outside. Examples are used to indicate how the different aspects of the space – physical, personal and cultural – can support or constrain children's activity. Once practitioners identify and reflect upon these aspects, they can make changes to the spaces in which they work and maximize the opportunities offered to children by being in outdoor learning environments. The model then becomes a rich mechanism for the development of outdoor learning environments that are fit for purpose.

The final section, Section 3, adopts an international perspective: it considers outdoor play in Scandinavia, New Zealand and Australia. The author of each chapter considers many of the themes addressed in previous chapters, in relation to early years settings in their country/culture. For example: the role of outdoor play in young children's lives, development and education; children's access to outdoor environments and the nature of these environments; what children do when outdoors; issues related to risky play and how the child is viewed in relation to risk.

Ellen Beate Hansen Sandseter considers outdoor play in Scandinavian countries, focusing particularly on developmental and educational outcomes as well as children's overall wellbeing. Outdoor play is discussed in the light of cultural norms and the development of education policy, both past and present. Scandinavian children's access to diverse outdoor environments and how these environments afford various forms of play is also considered. A particular focus of the chapter is the challenges and opportunities for risk-taking in play that outdoor environments give children, and how the child is viewed in relation to risk in Scandinavian countries.

New Zealanders' acceptance of the outdoors as an integral part of their way of life is reflected in the long-held commitment to ensuring young

children in early childhood education (ECE) centres have access to the outdoors as a learning environment. Alison Stephenson's chapter considers how,
despite this commitment, and the recognition of this shared cultural value
in the New Zealand early childhood curriculum, *Te Whāriki* (Ministry of
Education 1996), there are structural pressures which mean children's access
to the outdoors needs to be defended and the quality of outdoor environments
needs to be protected. In addition, Alison explores the professional discussions
and debates about the kinds of outdoor experiences children have access to
and how these debates indicate ways in which outdoor play provision may be
extended in the future.

In a final chapter that focuses on provision in Australia, Helen Little
and Shirley Wyver discuss Australian children's access to outdoor environments and practitioners' tolerance of risk-taking behaviours in outdoor play.
They present a critical argument that Australians have contradictory values
regarding outdoor environments. On the one hand, the Australian identity is
closely aligned with images of outdoor lifestyle and large expanses of natural
settings such as beaches and rainforests. On the other hand, most Australians
spend an increasing amount of time indoors or in vehicles and are wary of
the dangers of outdoor environments. The impact of these contradictory values on opportunities for children's outdoor play and learning in Australia are
explored.

Concluding thoughts

As we have indicated above, discourses and constructs that tend to be dominant within much of the western world – such as the 'innocent child' and that
of the 'unsafe outdoors' – as well as the demands of providing quality outdoor
experiences while addressing a statutory curriculum (or at least working
within a restrictive regulatory regime), are themes that are relevant across all
the chapters in this book. In interrogating these, readers may seek out their
own answers to the key issues set at the start of this chapter, namely:

- what constitutes 'good' outdoor provision for young children and
  babies;
- how we respect and respond to the young child in outdoor provision;
  and
- how we support risky play within the bounds of a statutory curriculum or a restrictive regulatory regime.

As editors, then, above all we hope that the book provokes critical reflection
and inspires the confidence to provide meaningful, engaging and challenging
outdoor spaces for young children's play and learning.

References

Anning, A., Cullen, J. and Fleer, M. (eds) (2009) *Early Childhood Education: Society and Culture*, 2nd edn. London: Sage.

Bailey, R. (2011) *Letting Children Be: Report of an Independent Review of the Commercialisation and Sexualisation of Childhood*. London: DfE.

Bilton, H. (2002) *Outdoor Play in the Early Years*, 2nd edn. London: David Fulton Publishers.

Dahlberg, G., Moss, P. and Pence, A. (1999) *Beyond Quality in Early Childhood Education and Care*. London: RoutledgeFalmer.

Danaher, G., Schirato, T. and Webb, J. (2000) *Understanding Foucault*. London: Sage.

DCELLS (2008) *The Foundation Phase Framework for Children's Learning Aged 3–7 in Wales*. Cardiff: Welsh Assembly Government.

DCELLS (2009) *The Outdoor Learning Handbook*. Cardiff: Welsh Assembly Government.

DfE (2012) *Early Years Foundation Stage*. Cheshire: Department for Education.

DfE (2013) *Archive: Learning Outside the Classroom Manifesto*. http://webarchive .nationalarchives.gov.uk/20130401151715/https://www.education.gov.uk/ publications/standard/publicationDetail/Page1/DFES-04232-2006 (accessed 3 October 2013).

DfES (2006) *Learning Outside the Classroom Manifesto*. Nottingham: Department for Education and Skills.

Early Years Interboard Panel (2005) *Learning Outdoors in the Early Years*. Belfast: Early Years Interboard Panel.

Education Scotland (2013) *Understanding the Curriculum*. http://www.education-scotland.gov.uk/thecurriculum/whatiscurriculumforexcellence/understand-ingthecurriculumasawhole/index.asp (accessed 3 October 2013).

Furedi, F. (2008) *Paranoid Parenting: Why Ignoring Experts May be Best for Your Child*. London: Continuum International Publishing Group.

Learning and Teaching Scotland (2010) *Curriculum for Excellence in the Outdoors*. Glasgow: Learning and Teaching Scotland.

Louv, R. (2010) *Last Child in the Woods: Saving our Children from Nature-deficit Disorder*. London: Atlantic Books.

Louv, R. (2013) *The Nature Principle: Human Restoration and the end of Nature-Deficit Disorder*. Chapel Hill, NC: Algonquin Books.

MacNaughton, G. (2005) *Doing Foucault in Early Childhood Studies: Applying Poststructural Ideas*. London: Routledge.

Maynard, T. (2007) Encounters with Forest School and Foucault: a risky business?, *Education 3–13*, 35(4): 379–91.

Maynard. T., Taylor, C., Waldron, S. et al. (2013a) *Evaluating the Foundation Phase: Policy Logic Model and Programme Theory*. Cardiff: Welsh Government Social Research. http://wales.gov.uk/about/aboutresearch/social/latestresearch/eval-uating-foundation-phase/?lang=en (accessed 6 January 2014).

Maynard, T., Waters, J. and Clement, J. (2013b) Child-initiated learning, the outdoor environment and the 'underachieving' child, *Early Years: An International Research Journal*, 33(3): 212–25.

Ministry of Education (1996) *Te Whāriki: Early Childhood Curriculum*. Wellington: Learning Media.

Moyles, J. (ed.) (2010) *The Excellence of Play*. Buckingham: Open University Press.

NIC (2006) *Northern Ireland Curriculum: Understanding the Foundation Stage*. Belfast: Early Years Interboard Publication

NIC (2013) *Areas of Learning at Foundation Stage*. http://www.nicurriculum.org.uk/foundation_stage/areas_of_learning (accessed 3 October 2013).

Palmer, S. (2007) *Toxic Childhood: How the Modern World is Damaging Our Children and What We Can Do About It*. London: Orion Books.

Taylor, A. (2013) *Reconfiguring the Natures of Childhood*. Oxon: Routledge.

Thomas, G. and Hocking, G. (2003) *Other People's Children*. London: DEMOS.

Welsh Government (2012) *Foundation Phase*. http://wales.gov.uk/topics/educationand-skills/earlyyearshome/foundation_phase/?lang=en (accessed 3 October 2013).

Welsh Government (2013) *National Literacy and Numeracy Framework*. Cardiff: Welsh Government.

Wood, E. (2013) *Play, Learning and the Early Childhood Curriculum*. London: Sage.

Section 1

The case for outdoor play

1 Outdoor play and the early years tradition

Helen Tovey

> *There should be a garden attached where they may feast their eyes*
> *on trees, flowers, and plants . . . where they always hope to hear and*
> *see something new.*
>
> *(Comenius, The Great Didactic 1632)*

Provision for gardens and outdoor play is a distinctive feature of an early childhood tradition spanning many centuries. To understand our contemporary ideas and practices we need to look at those in the past and particularly at significant pioneers of the early childhood tradition. This is not about glorifying the past as a golden era of good practice or trying to preserve outdated theories and practices. Nor is it about seeing the past as a series of mistakes from which we have evolved a more enlightened present. Rather it is about deepening our understanding of the roots of current ideas and practices in ways which can help us move forward with more strength and confidence. The past is an inescapable part of the present. Ideas and practices are not invented anew by each generation; rather, they evolve, losing parts here, gaining new emphasis there, some parts remaining buried to be re-discovered later with new impetus and meaning.

The ideas of the pioneers should rightly be placed in their historical and cultural contexts rather than seen out of context and viewed through our own twenty-first-century lens, a point argued strongly by Joyce (2012); however, it is also important to recognize that the pioneers themselves were challenging prevailing ideas of their time and in that sense were 'out of place' in their own cultural contexts. It is a reminder as well that ideas have developed not by people accepting 'what is' but being prepared to argue for an alternative vision of 'what could be'.

This chapter focuses on just four distinctive pioneers who have shaped our understanding of outdoor play: Friedrich Froebel, Maria Montessori, Margaret McMillan and Susan Isaacs. What were their perspectives on outdoor play?

Friedrich Froebel (1782–1852)

For Froebel the garden was central to his notion of 'kindergarten' – a place where children could grow and develop in harmony with nature. The first kindergarten opened in 1837 in Blankenburg, a small village close to the Thuringian mountains in what is now Germany. It was an inclusive kindergarten with children from different social classes and religions in contrast to the segregated schools of the time. Froebel created the word kindergarten rather than 'school' or 'institution', which implied more formal instruction. Rather he saw it as a community where children could grow and develop at their own pace, with adults who understood their development and cultivated their unique capacities just as good gardeners tend young plants. The garden then was both a literal place and a metaphorical idea representing Froebel's pedagogical vision. Along with key thinkers of his time such as philosopher Immanuel Kant, Froebel believed in a divine unity and connectedness between all living things and it was therefore important for children to be close to nature in the outdoor environment (Liebschner 1992).

The kindergarten included a garden area for play outdoors and space so that each child had their own plot of land for gardening. If there was not enough space, two children could share each plot as 'connections of twos in the kindergarten . . . teaches friendliness and each child is so much the richer for what the other puts in the bed' (Froebel cited in Herrington 1998: 33). Here children could sow seeds, tend the plants and harvest the produce, developing an awareness of the cycles of life and the changing seasons as well as interest in the insects and small creatures nearby. Children often gave the produce to the poorest members of the community, emphasizing the importance of caring for others and social responsibility.

The individual garden plots, each with their wooden name labels, were surrounded by a path and by communal plots for flowers, fruit and vegetables and for arable crops. Children could arrange and grow what they liked in their own plots but they had to work together in the communal gardens and take responsibility for them. This was no mere arrangement; rather, it illustrated in a tangible form Froebel's philosophy of unity between the parts and the whole, individual and community, freedom and responsibility. The individual was protected, even embraced, by the community but also had a responsibility to it. Freedom was tempered by responsibility (Liebschner 1992).

Through gardening and play outdoors children learnt about nature and about the growth of plants and animals but they also learnt to care for and to take responsibility for nature and gradually to recognize their own place in the natural world. Froebel believed that as children grew to respect and take care of living things so this led to a greater sense of self and others: 'The child who has cared for another living thing . . . is more easily led to care for his own life (Froebel, in Lilley 1967: 128). The garden was not a place for didactic lessons in nature study, or for teaching skills of horticulture. Rather children learnt through their own activity and experience. 'To have found one quarter of the answer by his own efforts is of more value and importance to the child than to half hear and half understand it in the words of others' (Froebel 1826: 86).

However, Froebel argued that self-activity was not sufficient on its own. It was important for children to represent their ideas in some form so they could become more aware of their own learning and 'know' about something in a deeper, more reflective way. Resources such as sticks, stones, leaves, chalk, sand and water were valuable materials for children to represent their ideas symbolically. Through the use of symbols children could innovate, imagine and create. Open-ended materials were significant as they could be transformed into a myriad of different forms and Froebel argued that 'as the material becomes less tangible, so there is a greater advance in creative expression' (Froebel, in Lilley 1967: 113).

Froebel's garden then was a spiritual place where children could grow and develop in harmony with nature. It was a place for creative and imaginative play, for investigation and discovery, for stories, songs, music, dance and games. Central to Froebel's philosophy was the belief in unity so that children experienced areas of learning in a connected and meaningful way, building on what is already known.

Maria Montessori (1869–1952)

Montessori was a qualified doctor, educator and campaigner working in Italy at the end of the nineteenth and beginning of the twentieth century. For Montessori it was not the garden but the 'house' which was the enduring metaphor for her approach to early childhood. The environment, she argued, should allow children to be like masters in their own houses; that is, it should be child sized, offer independent movement and be well organized with everything in its place. It was not nature but science and her notion of 'scientific pedagogy' which was a guiding principle. Using Froebel's metaphor of the gardener she argued that 'behind the good cultivator . . . stands the scientist'. Scientific knowledge helps not only to a better knowledge of the plants 'but can be used to transform them' (Montessori 1989: 9).

Montessori's first 'Children's House' was located in the poorest district of Rome. The garden was within a central courtyard surrounded by tenement flats and the space consisted of open areas for running and playing games with hoops, balls and ropes as well as gardens bordered with trees for shade. As in Froebel's garden there were individual plots for each child to plant and care for. Daily watering of the plants was one of the 'exercises of practical life' which Montessori advocated for developing children's independence and manual dexterity. Montessori saw nature as important for developing children's skill in observing natural life, a sense of responsibility, patience, an attitude of confident expectation and a sense of the wonder of nature. There was, she argued, nothing new in the idea of a garden for children: 'The novelty lies perhaps in my idea for the use of this space, which is to be in direct communication with the schoolroom so that children may be free to go and come as they like, throughout the entire day' (Montessori 1920: 81). It was Montessori, therefore, who pioneered the idea of open access from indoors to outdoors and free choice and self-direction. But 'choice' was restricted. The outdoor space was not a space for the imagination nor was it a space for play. 'If I were persuaded that children needed to play I would have provided the proper apparatus, but I am not so persuaded' (Montessori, cited in Bruce 1984: 80). Unlike Froebel who saw creativity, imagination and symbolic transformation as higher-level thinking, Montessori saw them as a distraction from real world understanding.

Montessori argued that structured materials which had been 'subject to the perfecting hand of a higher intelligence' (Montessori 1983: 47) were necessary to identify the 'real' or 'true' nature of the child. She devised a range of didactic apparatus to promote specific areas of learning which children could select independently and work on outside on a mat if they wished. Despite this freedom of choice and movement there was a particular tension between Montessori's idea of freedom and the restrictions she placed on such things as stories, creative imagination, and real world investigation and enquiry but it is a reminder that freedom is a porous term: it takes on the values of those who use it. It is freedom to 'do what' that matters.

Clearly Froebel and Montessori offered very different approaches to the garden although both valued gardening outdoors. Froebel valued exploration, investigation, music, dance, stories and symbolic play outdoors. Montessori valued focused attention on didactic apparatus, practical life and gymnastic exercises. Froebel emphasized imagination and creativity; Montessori emphasized real world understandings. Learning, Montessori believed, moved from the parts to the whole whereas Froebel believed the whole must be experienced first. Yet while Froebel was sometimes ambivalent about the degree of direction required, Montessori advocated free choice and movement indoors and out.

Margaret McMillan (1860–1931)

Margaret McMillan was a socialist politician, social reformer and campaigner working in England at a similar time to Montessori. Her experience of running an open-air camp for children in the slums of Deptford, South London where disease was rife convinced her that time spent outdoors could dramatically improve children's health, particularly for the youngest children. Following her successful 'night camps' where children slept outdoors to escape disease in their overcrowded homes, she developed an open-air nursery school for children. The specially designed and built garden was central to the school and the indoor spaces were merely shelters for use in very bad weather. Everything, she argued, could take place outdoors: play, sleep, meals, stories and games (McMillan 1919).

McMillan was a Froebelian and claimed to have nothing to do with Montessori; however, she was influenced, as was Montessori, by the didactic 'sense training' of the French physiologist and psychologist Eduard Seguin. She argued that there was no need for artificial didactic apparatus such as that used by Montessori to stimulate children's senses in isolation when real first-hand experience offered richer and more meaningful opportunities.

> Suppose you want to develop the touch sense! Lo! Here are a score of leaves, hairy sunflower, crinkled primrose, glossy fuchsia, and the rose. Do you want to compare colours, to note hues and shades? Well here is wealth a plenty. The herb garden will offer more scents than anyone can put into a box, and a very little thought will make of every pathway a riot of opportunities.
>
> (McMillan, cited in Bradburn 1989: 17)

As Bruce points out, 'the riot of opportunities and the real flowers rather than apparatus is more Froebelian in influence, while the 'you want to develop the touch sense' is influenced by the programmed approach of Seguin' (Bruce 1991: 47). Mention of 'scents in a box' is a probable reference to Montessori's sense training apparatus. McMillan's advice to adults to ask such questions as 'What is the biggest leaf in the garden? What colour is it? Show me the blue flowers' reflects the influence of Montessori's didactic approach. The two perspectives do not sit easily together and this tension is evident in aspects of her approach to the garden.

McMillan literally designed and built her garden for children, clearing and transforming a derelict site into a landscaped garden. The garden was arranged on different levels, on grass and hard surfaces and surrounded by trees. There were paths, steps, open spaces, logs, climbing bars, slides, banks, ropes, swings, shrubberies, sheds and playhouses. Everything was designed and provided for some reason. Steps for example were not just functional but provided important places for jumping on and off and provided valuable practice for 'little people who are learning to go up and down' (McMillan 1919: 49).

There was a horticulture section consisting of a herb garden, kitchen garden and rock garden and McMillan also included a wild garden arguing that 'children love a wilderness. So one plot should be allowed to grow wild but many beautiful things can be planted in it' (McMillan 1919: 47). The vegetables, fruits and herbs were harvested and used in the nursery kitchens in order to improve the children's diet. It is interesting to note that children helped the gardener grow the produce, rather than tend their own plots as in Froebel's garden; however, a patch of ground was available for digging and exploring.

There were areas for climbing and trees were considered 'the finest kind of apparatus for climbing you can ever have' (McMillan 1919: 23). Other areas provided opportunity for building and for imaginative play with boxes, wheels, ladders, planks, barrels and ropes. A wide range of animals, birds and aquatic life were provided including rabbits, guinea pigs, chickens and doves.

McMillan also included a junk heap: 'a nursery garden must have a free and rich place, a great rubbish heap, stones, and flints, bits of can, and old iron and pots. Here every healthy child will want to go, taking out things of his own choosing to build with' (McMillan 1919: 47). She noted that building houses in such a junk heap was 'the most popular activity after the making of mud hills and trenches and the filling of dams and rivers' (McMillan 1919: 76). These and other open-ended materials such as boxes, planks, ropes and wheels suggested that urban scrap or what are referred to as 'loose parts' today, were important features of provision which provoked children's interest and creativity.

McMillan recognized the supreme importance of health and wellbeing for children's development and learning. Children were rescued from their impoverished homes and placed in an open-air, sensory-rich environment; however, the garden was not isolated from the community but was central to the tenement buildings so that the gardens could be enjoyed by all and people could watch and learn about children's play. This idea of the garden as an important resource for the community was also emphasized by Froebel and Montessori. It raises the question, to what extent are nursery gardens a community resource today?

Susan Isaacs (1885–1948)

Susan Isaacs was a trained infant teacher, graduate in philosophy and psychology and a practising psychoanalyst. She worked in a very different social context from McMillan, an experimental school for highly advantaged children of professional parents in Cambridge. Malting House School was opened in 1924 and had two central aims: 'to stimulate the active enquiry of the children themselves rather than to teach them' and 'to bring within their immediate experience every range of fact to which their interests reached out' (Isaacs 1930: 17). Children were given considerable freedom, partly so that they could be studied under free conditions, but also because Isaacs argued that 'play has the greatest value for the child when it is really free and his own' (Isaacs 1929: 133).

The garden included a sand-pit and tap, space for making bonfires, a wooden climbing frame, slides, moveable ladders and an unusual see-saw with hooks and weights attached so children could weigh each other. There were fruit trees, flower and vegetable gardens with individual plots for each child and a range of animals including chickens, guinea pigs as well as snakes and salamanders.

A journalist from *The Spectator,* viewing a film about the school, provides a lively description of the Malting House garden.

> For a short half hour I watched children of from four to nine years of age having the time of their lives, wading up to their knees trying to fix a sandpit with water, mending a tap with a spanner, oiling the work of a clock, joyously feeding a bonfire, dissecting crabs, climbing on scaffolding, weighing each other on a seesaw . . . in fact doing all those things which every child delights in doing.
>
> (Cited in Graham 2009: 130)

The garden was a place for exploration, dramatic play, music, dance, songs, stories and games. It was a source of children's curiosity and enquiry which was supported and extended by adults. Together they investigated what burnt and what melted on the garden bonfire, explored the force of the water in the hosepipe, wondered whether the pilot of an overhead airplane might see or hear them and puzzled over the workings of the rainwater gutters and the waste water drains, to name but a few. A wide variety of open-ended materials supported a range of dramatic play scenarios outside including engines, trains, boats, battleships, fairy godmothers' palaces, giants and giant killers or whatever emerged from their experience, imagination and from stories.

The garden offered risk and challenge and children had considerable freedom to go wherever their curiosity led. But this freedom also had constraints. For example children were allowed to build and light fires but only one box of matches was given to each child and fires were not to be built near to the wooden summer house. Children were allowed to climb on the summer house roof but only one child was allowed at a time. They could use a range of gardening and woodwork tools like saws and hammers, but these were not to be used in a threatening manner and were always to be returned after use. Like Froebel and Montessori before her she argued that freedom brought responsibility but it also empowered children to develop the skills to be safe.

Isaacs' view of childhood was one of passion. Young children had a passion for finding out about and striving to understand the world. 'The thirst for understanding . . . springs from the child's deepest emotional needs . . . [it is] a veritable passion' (Isaacs 1932: 113). Isaacs saw children as whole beings and recognized their powerful emotions for she was not only an educator, but also a practising psychoanalyst and had trained with Melanie Klein. Play therefore was seen as an outlet for strong impulses, anxieties and emotions.

There was nothing soft or romantic about Isaacs' view of children and play. She noted children's raw, angry and sometimes destructive behaviour as well as their extreme gentleness and tenderness. The garden was also a safe place to express feelings of jealousy, hate, fear or anger. She noted when children's curiosity led them to pull worms in half, and she allowed them to dig up the dead pet rabbit when they wondered what had happened to it, but she did not allow any cruelty to living animals and firmly stopped them from harming a spider or stamping on insects. She acknowledged children's genuine curiosity about death so she and the children regularly dissected dead animals so that children could see and learn about the inner organs. Such practice might appear surprising or even shocking to some practitioners today. Yet it also challenges us to consider to what extent we pay attention to children's genuine enquiries including how and why things live and die, in our approach today.

Although she tried to observe children in free conditions she also recognized, unlike Montessori, that it was impossible to discover the 'natural child':

> Rather we have come to realise that most of the behaviour of children . . . in these years will be highly complex in its sources and springs. It will for instance always have some reference, implicit or explicit, to what adults expect – or to what children imagine that adults expect.
>
> (Isaacs 1930: 8)

Again this statement has relevance for practice today. What do adults expect outside and what do children think that adults expect?

Malting House School was open for only four years but its legacy has been long lasting. Isaacs' observations and meticulous documentation of children's behaviour, thinking and emotions are still a vibrant and rich resource today.

What is the essence of this tradition of outdoor play?

While there are clear differences in theory and practice amongst these pioneers of outdoor play, there are also common threads. Common to all the pioneers is an emphasis on the educative potential of the garden, nature and the wider environment. All in different ways valued free choice and movement, active engagement and first-hand meaningful experiences outdoors. Underpinning all their approaches was a respect for children, a view of children as competent, and trust in their growing abilities to do things for themselves in a challenging but supportive environment where the role of the adult is key. All but Montessori placed a strong emphasis on the creative and imaginative child and saw free play and talk as powerful vehicles for learning. Four of these themes, adventure, risk and challenge, nature and gardening, connecting with the wider environment and the significant role of the adult are now examined in more depth.

The importance of adventure, risk and challenge

These pioneers, in different ways, recognized children's desire for challenge and adventure. McMillan for example argued that children should 'play bravely and adventurously' in 'a provocative environment' (McMillan 1930: 78) Risk was seen as offering adventure and challenge rather than as a reason to stop children from doing something. Froebel, using the example of tree climbing, argued that we should focus on the benefits of the experience rather than on the risks. He suggested that,

> To climb a new tree is . . . to discover a new world; seen from above everything looks quite different from the usual telescoped, distorted side-view. If we could remember our joy when in childhood we looked out beyond the cramping limits of our immediate surroundings we should not be so insensitive to call out, 'Come down you will fall'.
>
> (Froebel, in Lilley 1967: 126)

He goes on to argue that children who experience increasing challenges in play are safer than those who have been protected from them because they gain a greater awareness of their own abilities as well as a greater ability to assess risks for themselves. Isaacs made a similar point when she addressed a safety conference in London arguing that, 'If you are going to keep children safe . . . you must provide places in which they can get the thrills they need; there must be trees they can climb and ways in which they can safely get the experience of adventure and the sense of challenge that they crave' (Isaacs 1938: 4).

In a contemporary climate often regarded as 'risk averse' with diminishing opportunities for young children to play outside, the value of children being able to do things for themselves, of learning the skills to do things safely and of developing a 'can do' attitude towards adventurous play outdoors has renewed importance (Tovey 2007). Understanding the ideas of the past can help challenge cultural constraints in the present and raise expectations of what children, with appropriate support, can do.

The value of contact with nature and gardening

For all the pioneers, working in very different social and economic conditions, intimate contact with nature was a rich source of learning for young children. Froebel and Isaacs in particular viewed the garden as a source of curiosity, enquiry and imaginative, creative and reflective thinking. Nature offered a source of beauty, a sense of harmony as well as a diverse, ever-changing environment. Contact with nature could be restorative, physically and emotionally. It taught children patience as nature takes its own time and cannot be hurried. Montessori emphasized the confident expectation which nature encourages. Isaacs valued nature for providing consistency, which could be very reassuring in children's sometimes emotionally turbulent worlds. Froebel emphasized the spiritual aspects of nature as well as the supreme importance of an ecological approach to the natural world. The moral dimension of taking responsibility for and caring for living things was emphasized by all the pioneers.

Today as children spend longer amounts of time indoors and are increasingly disconnected from the natural world (Louv 2006) the ideas of these pioneers have renewed importance and urgency. If children can engage with nature, see the effects of their actions on things around them and can get to know their own small garden including the plants and small creatures which inhabit it, in deep and meaningful ways, they can re-connect with nature and begin to see their own place within it.

Learning beyond the garden and connecting with the wider environment

The learning potential of the wider environment is emphasized by all the pioneers. Froebel for example believed that each kindergarten community should be connected with, not cut off from, the wider world of people and places. He suggested that for a toddler a walk outside is 'like a voyage of discovery and each new object is an America, a new world to explore' (Froebel, in Lilley 1967: 112). He urged all teachers to take their children outdoors 'not driving them like a flock of sheep or leading them as if a company of soldiers' but engaging in informal discussion about the things that interest them (Froebel, in Lilley 1967: 146). Froebel and children went out into the local areas and built dams in streams to investigate the flow of water and climbed hills to gain perspective on the surrounding landscapes (Liebschner 1992).

McMillan took children to the banks of the River Thames in London to see the boats, play with water and collect pebbles. Isaacs took children out and about in Cambridge, to the fens, to the river to investigate lock-gates and watermills, or to local streets to see road repairs, cable-laying and so on. Excursions were a means of extending children's particular interests and enquiries, opening up the wider world, both rural and urban, in ways the children could understand.

Such approaches resonate strongly with the contemporary notion of Forest School, where children are taken out on a regular basis to nearby woodland areas. Forest Schools have seen a resurgence of interest in the last decade or so but their roots can be found in Froebel's and other educators' use of local landscapes. Shields (2010) makes a strong case for acknowledging the historical roots of such educational approaches citing the woodcraft movement and Ernest Westlake's 'Forest School' which ran in Hampshire throughout the 1930s as examples of a strong tradition of outdoor education in the UK, rather than seeing Forest School as just a recent innovation from Denmark as is so often claimed.

The significant role of the adult

All of the pioneers saw adults as having a significant role outdoors. Froebel recognized the powerful impact that adults can have on children's dispositions to learn: 'Children who spend all their time in the open air may still observe nothing of its beauties. The boy sees the significance but if he does not find the same awareness in adults the seed of knowledge just beginning to germinate is crushed' (Froebel, in Lilley 1967: 146). The adult role, he argued, was complex but was to observe, to support children in finding answers to their own questions, to help children to reflect and to think for themselves, to help children make connections between different aspects of experience and to extend children's learning in sensitive ways (Tovey 2012).

Isaacs saw the adults' role as 'meeting the spontaneous enquiry of the children . . . and to give them the means of following these enquiries out in sustained and progressive action' (1930: 80). Planning was not based on pre-defined learning objectives, but was supremely responsive to children's interests and prevailing concerns.

Montessori argued for educators to trust children's growing competence, to give them time, freedom of movement and choice within a prepared environment. She emphasized the need for adult restraint in intervening or interrupting children. 'Teaching shall be vigorously guided by the principle of limiting to the greatest possible point the active intervention of the teacher' (Montessori 1920: 233). Although she saw this as an enabling rather than a passive role, it is possible that this approach may have been misinterpreted by some practitioners in subsequent generations as one where adults stand back and supervise. There is certainly evidence of some ambiguity and misapprehension in practitioners' perspectives on the purpose and value of outdoor play and the adult role; see for example Maynard and Waters (2007) and Bilton (2012).

Many of the pioneers' ideas can be seen in the Board of Education report on infant and nursery education in England and Wales (The Hadow Report) of 1933. Isaacs and Montessori gave evidence to the committee, Froebel's ideas are evident and McMillan's practice is referenced. The report argued that children in the nursery and infant years should spend a large proportion of their time out of doors:

> The open air provides the best environment for physical well-being, but this is not the only reason why the children in the infant school should spend a large part of their school hours out of doors. Not the home, nor the school, but the unroofed country is the child's natural laboratory or workshop where he finds the things that appeal to his primitive instincts, the plants, flowers, bushes, living animals, stream, moveable earth or sand, that are his raw material for experience and experiment. The field, the park, the garden, the woodland copse, the waste patch, all are full of interesting things which will hold the child's eye, arouse his wonder, stimulate his enquiries, give opportunities for discovery. It is here, from observation of real things and happenings, that the foundations are best laid of most of the branches of knowledge which will be studied in later school life.
>
> (Board of Education 1933: 125)

This is a powerful statement about the importance of outdoor learning; however, the report argued for an eclectic approach combining features from very different pedagogical approaches. Such an approach can create ambiguity and uncertainty particularly in relation to the adult role. Webb, commenting on the decline of the rich nursery tradition, argued that ideas once at variance began to merge, leading to practices which were 'attenuated shadows of what they originally were' and often reduced to the 'lowest common denominator' (Webb 1974: 54). It is not hard to find examples of practice today which are far removed from the ideas of the pioneers, where learning is driven by outcomes and targets rather than children's powerful urge to learn or where outdoor play takes place in flat, sterile, safety-surfaced playgrounds, cut off from the natural world or from authentic first-hand experiences.

Summary

At a time of renewed focus on play and learning outdoors re-examining the principles of the pioneers helps us to reflect critically on our own perspectives on the purpose and value of outdoor play and the principles which underpin the use of the outdoor space. Is it a place of passionate enquiry, with adults who support children's curiosity and investigation? Is it a place for adventurous and challenging play? Is it a place where creativity and imagination flourish? How does it connect with the community and the wider world? What are the freedoms that we want for children and what constraints best allow those freedoms to thrive? Specifically, what is the adult role and what do children think is the adult's role outdoors?

Looking at historical traditions offers a variety of lenses through which to view our own ideas and practices. What better testament to the pioneers of the past than to revisit their ideas, use them to reflect on the present, to question, challenge, affirm and ultimately strengthen our pedagogical principles and approaches in ways which will enrich our thinking and help shape vibrant opportunities for outdoor play in the future.

References

Bilton, H. (2012) The type and frequency of interactions that occur between staff and children outside in Early Years Foundation Stage settings, *European Early Childhood Education Research Journal*, 20(3): 403–21.

Board of Education (1933) *Report of the Consultative Committee on Infant and Nursery Schools (Hadow Report)*. London: HMSO.

Bradburn, E. (1989) *Margaret McMillan: Portrait of a Pioneer*. London: Routledge.

Bruce, T. (1984) A Froebelian look at Montessori's work, *Early Child Development and Care*, 19(3): 151–73.

Bruce, T. (1991) *Time to Play in Early Childhood Education*. London: Hodder & Stoughton.

Froebel, F. (1826) *Education of Man* (trans. W. Hailmann 1908). New York: Appleton & Co.

Graham, P. (2009) *Susan Isaacs. A Life Freeing the Minds of Children*. London: Karnac Books.

Herrington, S. (1998) The garden in Froebel's Kindergarten: beyond the metaphor, *Studies in the History of Gardens and Designed Landscapes*, 18(4): 326–38.

Isaacs, S. (1929) *The Nursery Years. The mind of the child from birth to six years*. London: Routledge & Kegan Paul.

Isaacs, S. (1930) *Intellectual Growth in Young Children*. London: Routledge & Kegan Paul.

Isaacs, S. (1932) *The Children We Teach*. London: Routledge & Kegan Paul.

Isaacs, S. (1938) Lecture to National Safety Congress, *National Froebel Foundation Bulletin* (1960), no. 125. London: National Froebel Foundation.

Joyce, R. (2012) *Outdoor Learning Past and Present*. Maidenhead: Open University Press.

Lilley, I. (1967) *Friedrich Froebel: A Selection From His Writings*. Cambridge: Cambridge University Press.

Liebschner, J. (1992) *A Child's Work: Freedom and Guidance in Froebel's Educational Theory and Practice*. Cambridge: Lutterworth Press.

Louv, R. (2006) *Last Child in the Woods: Saving our Children from Nature-Deficit Disorder*. New York: Algoriquin Books.

McMillan, M. ([1919] 1930) *The Nursery School*. London: Dent.

Maynard, T. and Waters, J. (2007) Learning in the outdoor environment: a missed opportunity, *Early Years*, 27(3): 255–65.

Montessori, M. (1920) *The Montessori Method*. London: Heineman.

Montessori, M. (1983) *The Secret of Childhood*. London: Sangan Books Ltd.

Montessori, M. (1989) *The Formation of Man*. Oxford: Clio Press Ltd.

Shields, P. (2010) Forest School: reclaiming it from Scandinavia, *FORUM* 52(1), available at www.wwwords.co.uk/FORUM (accessed 5 April 2013).

Tovey, H. (2007) *Playing Outdoors: Spaces and Places, Risk and Challenge*. Maidenhead: Open University Press.

Tovey, H. (2012) *Bringing the Froebel Approach to Your Early Years Practice*. London: Routledge.

Webb, L. (1974) *Purpose and Practice in Nursery Education*. Oxford: Blackwell.

2 What makes a good outdoor environment for young children?

Jan White and Helen Woolley

> *Children are born passionately eager to make as much sense as they can of things around them . . . if we attempt to control, manipulate, or divert this process . . . the independent scientist in the child disappears.*
>
> *(John Holt 1990: 95)*

This chapter starts by discussing what is meant by a good outdoor environment for children in their early years, suggesting what such an environment should provide. We then go on to draw upon a range of academic disciplines, including psychology, landscape architecture, play and early years education, to discuss the characteristics of a good outdoor environment. Finally we summarize future directions for thinking and research.

We acknowledge that play is a main way that children learn and that we are writing from a UK perspective. In addition we draw upon the theories of affordance (Gibson 1979), habitat, which will be woven into the text (Appleton 1975), and schema, which will now be briefly explained.

Schemas (Athey 1990) are recognized as repeated patterns in children's play behaviours as they interact with, explore and build theories about their world: 'Schemas are integrated, coordinated networks of behaviour through which children can gain access to knowledge and understanding, and sort out their ideas, feelings and relationships. They are part of the way the child's brain is wired' (Bruce 2005: 90). Schema theory is a highly useful lens through which to observe and consider the significance of children's actions and behaviours as they focus on particular content and processes (threads or schemas) in their environment, grapple with some big ideas about how their world operates and build their own thinking tools. Athey (1990) maintains that a child's schema can be seen as at the core of the developing mind and thus a central element of intellectual growth. It is therefore important, as Nutbrown (2011) indicates, that educational experiences are related to this core.

What is a 'good' outdoor environment for young children?

The field of environmental psychology has established that the environment has a strong influence on feelings, mood, behaviour, action and experience (Prescott 2008). Within early childhood education it is acknowledged that the environment is a critical pedagogical element, with the indoor environment often being referred to as the 'third teacher' (Ceppi and Zini 1998). Indeed it could be argued that the environment is the 'first teacher' because its influence, working at an evolutionary and subconscious level, is profound and both immediate and long lasting; however, the quality of outdoor spaces is often far from good in the UK, revealing little understanding of young children, their well-being and developmental needs both in existing and newly provided outdoor spaces. Outdoor environments in educational settings have been less studied than those indoors for their pedagogical role.

What do we mean by a 'good' outdoor environment? A useful starting point is to reflect upon current notions of what these places should provide and therefore could look like. In an educational context, whose agenda(s) should we be working to in these places?

Critically, we must investigate our own and society's values about children, childhood and education: What is education? What is it for? What is the role of early childhood educators? If the outdoor environment is going to be a really 'good' environment, what would make it both powerful and empowering for children? The external environment can send messages, known as the hidden curriculum, that children will feel, internalize and come to believe about themselves (Titman 1994). Therefore it is important that we articulate the messages that we *want* this environment to be giving and constantly refer to these to underpin decisions about space, layout, materials, organization, day-to-day routines and minute-by-minute practice and interaction.

Working from the theoretical perspective that children 'inhabit' a space, and through their actions the space becomes a place, we can consider the environment as a 'habitat'. If this is to be a 'good' habitat for young children we need to find out what it feels like to be in this place (Hart 1979; Clark and Moss 2005), and what signals the characteristics of this environment send to them. What do they see in their environment? What does it do to them? How do they respond? Working from attending to what young children want and need to do, we now explore what qualities, characteristics and features best afford this.

Characteristics of a good outdoor environment

When considering a good outdoor environment for young children from birth to 7 years old we suggest, informed by the literature, a series of six interlinking concepts: physically diverse, generous, supportive, secure, agency and connection. Within each concept different and sometimes overlapping characteristics are identified.

Physically diverse: for being whole-bodied and fully physical

Research by Fjørtoft and colleagues has identified that diversity in landscape elements such as vegetation and topography contribute to a good outdoor environment for young children. Their studies indicated that such landscape features met children's needs for a stimulating and varied play environment, positively influenced the range and levels of physical activity, and improved children's motor development and fitness (Fjørtoft and Sageie 2000; Fjørtoft 2004). A three-dimensional, layered approach to the design of the outdoor environment is recommended by Shaw (1987) so that 'spaces, places, platforms and paths interact vertically. This stacking will maximise physical, verbal and visual interactions between users' (p. 202). Elements that can be used to link overlapping planes also offer rich opportunity to introduce physical variety.

Slopes, steps, terraces and other level changes, such as low trees for clambering, increase the affordance for movement and play potential and provide great provocation for use of the body. This has considerable influence on developmental processes such as locomotion skills (Olds 1987; Olds 2000) and visual perception (Gibson 1979). It also stimulates neurological systems involved in balance, body sense and cross-lateral linkage, which give a child control and confidence in space and gravity (Jabadao 2005; Goddard Blythe 2009). Simply moving over a varied terrain feeds complex sensory information into the brain, enabling the child to 'calibrate' him or herself against the environment as they grow and develop (Hughes 2001; White 2011).

Raised surfaces offer children a new perspective on their environment, often causing comments like, 'I can see the whole world from here!' For young children being high up in a 'look-out' can elicit feelings of exhilaration, power and a sense of control (Hayward 1993). Such common responses to environmental features can be understood through the lens of 'habitat theory' (Appleton 1975), in which preferences for particular landscape features are seen to correspond with an evolutionarily ancient and deep-seated psychological drive to ensure that our survival needs are met. In this context 'prospect' enables us to survey the landscape for orientation, danger and sources of food and water. Overlooking and looking-on are also important precursors to children joining in a play activity (Shaw 1987).

Value for play and development can be provided by a range of different surfaces beyond the limited opportunities of tarmac and rubber carpet (Woolley and Lowe 2013). Surfaces that offer variety and unpredictability, are uneven and bumpy, loose and 'give' under foot, or change in nature across boundaries are of benefit because they require different use of the body, increase attention that must be paid, and provide further challenge to balance and motor skills

(Adolf et al. 2003; Kranowitz 2005). If children have the opportunity to move over such diverse surfaces with bare feet, sensory input is greatly increased and full use of the foot in locomotion is supported (Howell 2010: 44–5).

A 'high-mobility' environment (Prescott 2008) supports the young child to learn about gravity and three-dimensional space, their body's relationship to the ground and how the physical world works, and can lead to exceptional physical and intellectual inventiveness (White 2010).

Generous: for enquiry, discovery and thinking

The kinds of materials and resources available to young children in the outdoor environment, together with the ways they are supported to make use of them, can significantly affect the nature of their experiences: '[The child] needs a generous environment, generous in warmth of feeling, and in opportunity for activity. He needs appropriate materials to work on and an attitude of encouragement and eagerness in those who work with him' (Isaacs 1954: 21). Isaacs identified three kinds of generosity (Rich et al. 2008):

- a rich 'treasure chest' of an *environment*, with an abundance of interesting 'stuff' for children to handle;
- the availability of *'big ideas'* – investigating and making sense of the real world;
- an abundance of *time* for doing and thinking that is uninterrupted and not pre-structured.

For young children it is especially important to have materials, resources and equipment that are 'open' (Prescott 2008). Open-ended, non-prescribed materials in the outdoor environment, such as sand, water, vegetation and other natural materials, are versatile, adaptable and responsive to whatever the child wants to do. They are also valuable as 'transitional objects' on the way towards symbolic thought, being able to stand in the place of something else as symbolic representations, and thus becoming tools for thinking (Medina 2008). 'Children possess a natural *openness* to the potential of materials . . . The goal is to allow children to become fluent with materials – as if materials were a language' (Topal and Gandini 1999). Loose materials can be handled, carried and moved around the outdoor space, and relocated from place to place. Resources that are large, heavy and awkward to manipulate support the development of body awareness and control through stimulating the proprioceptive sensory system (Kranowitz 2005). Mobile materials also provide rich content for developing big ideas (theories) about space, place and relationship through schemas such as transporting, trajectories, enclosing, placing, connecting and going through boundaries (Athey 1990; Nutbrown 2011). Such activity also contributes to developing embodied understandings of concepts such as quantity, distance, weight and capacity.

The term 'loose parts' originally referred to more than the fact that elements were simply mobile – that of intentionally planning for a large number of *variables* in the environment. Variables change and can be changed by the playing child, and can also interact with each other.

> There is evidence that all children love to interact with variables, such as materials and shapes; smells and other physical phenomena (such as electricity, magnetism and gravity); media such as gases and fluids; sounds, music, motion; chemical interactions, cooking and fire; and other humans, and animals, plants, words, concepts and ideas. With all these things all children love to play, experiment, discover and invent and have fun.
>
> (Nicholson 1971: 30)

If there are plenty of suitable variables present in a child's environment, Nicholson suggested that the player will be more likely to engage in explorative behaviour and innovation – and thus investigate the big ideas recommended by Susan Isaacs: 'In any environment, both the degree of inventiveness and creativity, and the possibility of discovery, are directly proportional to the number and kind of variables in it. Environments should not be clean, static and impossible to play around with' (Nicholson 1971: 30).

In addition to a rich range of materials and variables, children will need copious amounts of time to follow their self-motivated enquiries, supported by sensitive and attuned adults who do not intrude on, disrupt or divert children's lines of thinking.

Supportive: for feeling nurtured, calm and imaginative

Young children can change energy levels rapidly, experiencing a sudden need for withdrawal, rest and recovery. The provision of suitable environmental features and qualities to support withdrawal, seclusion, downtime, peace and restoration should be considered as a critical dimension of a good outdoor environment.

'Softness' (Prescott 2008) is a characteristic that should pervade the whole environment. It is provided through the presence of materials which are responsive to one's body, such as sand, water, grass, swingseats, hammocks, rugs and, importantly, adult laps to sit on. The common characteristic of these soft materials is that they provide experiences where the environment responds to the child: they can use their body as they want to and the material responds by doing what they want it to do. Inhabitants of hard environments experience tension and fatigue. Softness is also important for the adults in the environment, so that they too feel nurtured and relaxed.

Softness in the outdoor environment helps to induce a state of calm and contemplation, noticed by Margaret McMillan in her younger nursery children in the early 1900s: 'The children stand watching, watching, with lax muscles, in that state of reverie which we note in them every day, and which is becoming to us a condition as well defined and deserving of respect as sleep. Perception takes *time*.' (McMillan [1919] 1930: 75). This state of 'reverie' is an important mode for creative thinking and may have a significant psychological role (Claxton 1997). Research on natural environments also shows the importance of providing a restorative environment for attention recovery (Kaplan and Kaplan 1989).

Prescott also identified the need for children to find places where they can withdraw, feel secure by not being intruded upon, have opportunities for seclusion and privacy, and exert control: thus relaxing the state of alertness and high cortisol levels that may be present in a busy group care environment (Prescott 2008). It is thus especially important that children can find or make places where they can be alone at times or with one or two friends or an adult.

A universal aspect of children's play is the making of small-sized hidey-holes and dens (Sobel 2002). These places are self made, personal, homely and under the child's control. 'To put up some kind of house, to fix some kind of tent and to sit inside – that is the aim of and desire of all the children' (McMillan [1919] 1930: 26).

These features also provide material for exploring several schemas, such as envelopment, enclosure, containment and boundaries, and are therefore very rich contexts for cognitive as well as emotional work (Bruce 2005; Nutbrown 2011).

Through the lens of evolutionary biology and habitat theory (Appleton 1975) personal place-making and den play can be understood as a manifestation of the need for a 'refuge' that is secret and hidden from predators. Such places give security and pleasurable sensations because they meet deep survival needs and calm the limbic part of the brain where emotions are processed. This safe haven is created by a combination of refuge – being held and hidden – and prospect – being able to look out for approaching danger. These are clear attributes in children's den play expressed in activities such as watching out for the wolves or the baddies (Kirkby 1989).

Secure: for feeling comfortable and at home

Within an outdoor environment that has variety, diversity, change and chance, it is critical that the child feels secure, can make good sense of the space and everything in it, and is able to predict what might happen. Too much stimulation, especially when not in the control of the child, can result in an overwhelmed, uncertain and even fearful child. Engagement and motivation occur where the environment feels familiar, makes sense to the learner and is easy to use. Thus children need to know, understand and read the outdoor environment, and for this to happen it needs to be stable and mappable, to become readable and predictable (Olds 1987). 'Everything somehow [needs] to fit together in a comprehensible way – to have a *rich normality*' (Greenman 2007: 84). There are particular aspects in organization and design that can provide variety within a framework of predictability, enabling young children to harness the richness of the outdoor environment. These aspects should include consideration of transition, storage and paths.

The interface between the indoor and outdoor halves or parts of the learning environment is an important physical and psychological space (Greenman 2007). Consideration should be given to how this 'transition zone' supports children to cross the threshold to go out or to come in, to move easily between inside and outside, to alter their behaviour between the two different environments, and to link their play and learning across them. Early years settings should have a vision of creating a transition space that works well for children and adults, that helps indoors and outdoors work in a joined up way, and which also captures the particular nature of this half-in and half-out 'third' space as a tranquil place.

The way in which resources are stored and made available to children also makes a major contribution to familiarity and ease of use. In an enabling environment, children should be able to self-select resources from a stable source and to access them independently (the *continuous provision* approach; Marsden and Woodbridge 2005). This is likely to require ample storage, and organization that seeks to make resources highly visible and accessible as individual items to children, arranged in a way that makes sense to the users.

A well-linked system of pathways can unify all parts of the outdoor environment, connecting them physically and spatially, allowing play to flow from place to place and enabling all areas to play their part. This 'linkage' (Shaw 1987) and 'connectivity' (Herrington and Lesmeister 2006) allows a complex environment, rich in variety of spaces and places, to be mapped out by the users through linking key places or landmarks and following routes, so that it becomes readable and predictable. This in turn allows the child to feel comfortable, able to make the most of the environment and at home in it. Harding (2005) found that journeying, physical play, transporting and imaginative play along pathways all help children to get to know their outdoor space and develop their spatial understanding of it. Children became secure through knowing the place and its places, and this formed part of constructing a sense of place, ownership and belonging.

Agency: for being in control and feeling powerful

A 'good' outdoor environment must meet the individual needs of every child inhabiting it, enable each child to construct their own play and follow their own enquiries, and give them a sense of control and empowerment or agency. The group of characteristics in this section can contribute significantly to creating such an empowering environment.

As well as flexibility in resources, 'flexibility' or openness in how the environment can be used and manipulated itself brings higher play value and valuable educational outcomes (Shaw 1987). In her work where both resources and how they could be used were open and undetermined, Broadhead (2004) found that such manipulable, child-determined spaces had higher levels of developmental value, with:

- more complex social interaction and negotiation;
- new dimensions of friendship;
- more meaningful and sustained play themes.

Both Margaret McMillan and Susan Isaacs understood the value of these characteristics – indeed McMillan recommended that nurseries should provide a 'junk heap': 'A Nursery Garden must have a free and rich place, a great rubbish heap, stones, flints, bits of can, and old iron and pots. Here every healthy child will want to go; taking out things of his own choosing to build with' (1919: 47).

Playwork researchers consider that flexibility in the play environment leads to increased flexibility in the child through a positive feedback cycle that is accumulative, called 'compound flexibility' (Hughes 2001; Brown 2003). Thus the environment itself supports development, in the child's own way and pace:

> The degree of flexibility in the play environment has a direct effect on a child's opportunities for experimentation, because it governs the level of control that the child is able to exercise. The freedom to experiment, where it exists, produces positive feelings, a sense of achievement, pleasure, etc. This in turn encourages the development of self-confidence, self-acceptance, etc. With increased self-confidence, the child becomes more comfortable with taking risks and consequently their reaction to day-to-day problems becomes more varied. This increasingly flexible approach to problem solving makes the child better able to use the full potential of the play environment [its affordance]. Thus the child moves closer to their developmental potential than would otherwise have been the case.
>
> (Brown 2003: 57)

Beyond flexibility, 'plasticity' is a characteristic where the environment is designed so that it can respond to the players – they can modify, mould and control it to make it their own. Plasticity refers to how *impressionable* the setting is (Kirkby 1989). The child shapes the environment and is in turn shaped by it. This responsiveness is a key to engagement and motivation as the environment has greater ability to draw and keep the child's deep involvement (Striniste and Moore 1989). Flexibility, plasticity and responsiveness are characteristics of an enabling environment where children are not simply 'readers' of what they are supposed or expected to do. By making their own spaces and structures children become architects of their environment and 'authors' of their play in it (Tovey 2007).

> The outdoor environment for young children is a dynamic, living place. . . . It is a domain that takes shape as children, or children and adults, inhabit it. Children interact with the environment almost like a play partner, shaping and transforming it, but in turn being shaped by the experiences and interactions it enables. . . . Children, then, should be 'authors', as well as 'readers' of their environments.
>
> (Tovey 2007: 54)

Through constructing an environment conducive to their own play, children become more creative, deepening their explorations and accessing even more of the environment's affordances. This 'authorship' is a strong notion that helps us to design and operate an outdoor environment that is motivational, empowering and richly developmental. Children inhabiting such a responsive and impressionable environment experience themselves as active *agents*: constructing and controlling their play environment, creating and conducting the flow of their play and in so doing, assembling their own spirits, minds and bodies.

Agency is considered to be a critical component of wellbeing and learning (Roberts 2010) and is vital if children are to become resilient, capable, confident and self-assured (DfE 2012). It is rooted in what Suransky (1982) has termed 'history-making power': 'They have the power to imprint themselves upon the landscape, endow their landscape with significance and experience their own activity as capable of transforming the environment' (Haas 1996: 350). An outdoor environment that is designed, managed and operated to focus on plasticity, responsiveness and authorship will be one that is both powerful and empowering for every child inhabiting it.

Connection: for travelling, journeying and adventure

Pathways exert a powerful influence on people, especially children, and can play a significant and multi-faceted role in how an outdoor environment operates for the people inhabiting it. Pathways constitute a component of habitat theory (Appleton 1975) in the form of tracks and trails, tugging on a natural inclination to follow where others have gone before: a safe route that may well lead to a source of interest. Pathways produce mixed emotions, depending upon their characteristics. When wide and straight, they can provide a sense of direction, expectation or destination. With a varying route or as stepping stones, they can offer changing perspectives or instill calm and reverie (Moore 1986; Hayward 1993). Alternatively, they can create a feeling of mystery, or even the sense of imagination and adventure that many practitioners say is missing from their outdoor space:

> The well-designed path is irresistible. It invites, even pulls people into the garden. Put a curve into a path that disappears around a corner and [people] will yearn to know what is around that corner. [Paths make the] garden become coherent while simultaneously offering intrigue, surprise, movement, variety and ever-changing perspectives.
> (Hayward 1993: 5)

Paths are often used in role play (Harding 2005), perhaps offering imagination, mystery and adventure. Children particularly value unofficial and hidden paths, connecting parts of their territories via routes adults might not think of using; their special way or short-cut (Moore 1986). They can also be made more complex by including steps, arches, tunnels and bridges, or by diverging and converging to encourage choice and decision making.

Paths make children move, so they can play a powerful role in the pedagogic outdoor environment in that they can support several schematic themes commonly seen in the early years, especially:

- *trajectory* schema, where movement in lines, arcs or curves is explored, building the child's ability to think about space and how movement can occur in it;
- *transporting* schema where children are physically experiencing movement and distance, length travelled and speed, through moving themselves and objects;
- *going through* schema, with the physical experience of going through and emerging at the other side (especially in tunnels and bridges);
- pathways with junctions and choices could support *grid* and *connecting* schematic interests.

Directions for outdoor environments in early childhood education

The significance of particular characteristics that make an outdoor play environment enjoyable, effective and deeply satisfying for young children, and the adults working with them, needs to be raised in design and development processes and use of these spaces. In order to create powerful pedagogical outdoor environments that enable foundational development and are appropriate places for young children's wellbeing, play and learning, we must move away from recent paradigms for outdoor play spaces, primarily of playgrounds, and provide outdoor spaces that aim to meet emotional and cognitive psychological and bodily needs.

Indications for the direction for productive thinking are as follows:

- We need to recognize the value of schema for deep physical and cognitive development and harness this theory as a design tool in young children's environments.
- A shift in thinking is needed, away from structured design towards semi-structured environments (Haas 1996) and design that harnesses the natural order and serendipity of nature.
- We must design, plan and operate for flexibility and increasingly flexible use, extending the 'enabling environments' discourse towards empowering and potentiating environments that support children's agency and 'history making power' (Suransky 1982).
- There should be an emphasis upon the creation of a three-dimensional environment and a movement-rich landscape (or 'terrain') for neurological and perceptive development.
- Increased vegetation and access to a wide range of natural elements and processes are needed (Herrington and Studtmann 1998).
- Future research could usefully address the influence and effective operation of transition zones and continuous provision of resources.

Much of the useful research is more than twenty years old (e.g. Shaw 1987; Striniste and Moore 1989) and/or focuses on the middle years (ages 7–12) of childhood (e.g. Moore 1986; Sobel 2002). Although this research is valuable, it needs to be updated and linked to current knowledge and discourses. In particular, we need research in the context of present early childhood programmes and practice. Outdoor environments need to be researched as places for wellbeing, learning and development, and for children to experience mixed-age play. Their potential for developing the citizens who have the desire, sense of agency and creativity to live well as a democracy and reside on our planet sustainably is also of great interest.

References

Adolf, K., Vereijken, B. and Shrout, P. (2003) What changes in infant walking and why, *Child Development*, 74(2): 475–97.

Appleton, J. (1975) *The Experience of Landscape*. New York: John Wiley and Sons.

Athey, C. (1990) *Extending Thought in Young Children: A Parent-Teacher Partnership*. London: Paul Chapman Publishing.

Blythe, S.G. (2009) *Attention, Balance and Coordination*. Chichester: Wiley-Blackwell.

Broadhead, P. (2004) *Early Years Play and Learning: Developing Social Skills and Cooperation*. London: RoutledgeFalmer.

Brown, F. (ed.) (2003) *Playwork: Theory and Practice*. Buckingham: Open University Press.

Bruce, T. (2005) *Early Childhood Education*, 3rd edn. London: Hodder Arnold.

Ceppi, G. and Zini, M. (eds) (1998) *Children, Spaces, Relations: Metaproject for an Environment for Young Children*. Italy: Reggio Children.

Clark, A. and Moss, P. (2005) *Spaces to Play: More Listening to Young Children Using the Mosaic Approach*. London: National Children's Bureau.

Claxton, G. (1997) *Hare Brain, Tortoise Mind: Why Intelligence Increases When You Think Less*. London: Fourth Estate.

DfE (2012) *Statutory Framework for the Early Years Foundation Stage*. Runcorn: Department for Education.

Fjørtoft, I. (2004) Landscape as playscape: the effects of natural environments on children's play and motor development, *Children, Youth and Environments*, 14(2): 21–44.

Fjørtoft, I. and Sageie, J. (2000) The natural environment as a playground for children: landscape description and analyses of a natural landscape, *Landscape and Urban Planning*, 48(1–2): 83–97.

Gibson, J.J. (1979) *The Ecological Approach to Visual Perception*. London: Lawrence Erlbaum.

Greenman, J. (2007) *Caring Spaces, Learning Places: Children's Environments That Work*. Redmond, WA: Exchange Press.

Haas, M. (1996) Children in the junkyard, *Childhood Education*, 72(6): 345–50.

Harding, S. (2005) Outdoor play and the pedagogic garden. In J. Moyles (ed.) *The Excellence of Play*. Maidenhead: Open University Press.

Hart, R. (1979) *Children's Experience of Place*. New York: Irvington Publishers Inc.

Hayward, G. (1993) *Garden Paths: Inspiring Designs and Practical Projects*. Charlotte, VT: Camden House Publishing.

Herrington, S. and Lesmeister, C. (2006) The design of landscapes at child-care centres: Seven Cs, *Landscape Research*, 31(1): 63–82.

Herrington, S. and Studtmann, M.K. (1998) From yard to garden: new directions in the design of children's outdoor play environments, *Landscape and Urban Planning*, 42: 191–205.

Holt, J. (1990) *Learning All the Time; how small children learn to read, write, count and investigate the world around them without being taught*. Cambridge, Mass: Da Capo Press.

Howell, D. (2010) *The Barefoot Book*. Alameda, CA: Hunter House Inc. Publishers.

Hughes, B. (2001) *Evolutionary Playwork and Reflective Analytic Practice*. Abingdon: Routledge.

Isaacs, S. (1954) *The Educational Value of the Nursery School*. London: BAECE.

Jabadao (2005) *Developmental Movement Play Full Report*. Leeds UK: National Centre for Movement, Learning and Health.

Kaplan, R. and Kaplan, S. (1989) *The Experience of Nature: A Psychological Perspective*. Cambridge: Cambridge University Press.

Kirkby, M. (1989) Nature as refuge in children's environments, *Children's Environments Quarterly*, 6(1): 7–12.

Kranowitz, C.S. (2005) *The Out-of-Sync Child: Recognizing and Coping with Sensory Processing Disorder*. New York: Skylight Press.

Marsden, E. and Woodbridge, J. (2005) *Looking Closely at Learning and Teaching: A Journey of Development*. Huddersfield: Early Excellence Ltd.

McMillan, M. ([1919] 1930) *The Nursery School*. London: Dent.

Medina, J. (2008) *Brain Rules: 12 Principles for Surviving and Thriving at Work, Home and School*. Seattle, WA: Pear Press.

Moore, R.C. (1986) *Childhood's Domain: Play and Place in Child Development*. London: Croom Helm.

Nicholson, S. (1971) How not to cheat children: the theory of loose parts, *Landscape Architecture*, October: 30–4.

Nutbrown, C. (2011) *Threads of Thinking*, 4th edn. London: Sage Publications Ltd.

Olds, A. (1987) Designing settings for infants and toddlers. In C.S. Weinstein and G.D. Thomas (eds) *Spaces for Children: The Built Environment and Child Development*. New York: Plenum.

Olds, A.R. (2000) *Childcare Design Guide*. New York: McGraw-Hill Professional.

Prescott, E. (2008) The physical environment: a powerful regulator of experience, *Exchange*, March/April: 34–7.

Rich, D., Drummond, M.J. and Myer, C. (2008) *Learning: What Matters to Children*. Clopton Suffolk: Rich Learning Opportunities.

Roberts. R. (2010) *Wellbeing From Birth*. London: Sage Publications.

Shaw, L.G. (1987) Designing playgrounds for able and disabled children. In C.S. Weinstein and G.D. Thomas (eds) *Spaces for Children: The Built Environment and Child Development*. New York: Plenum.

Sobel, D. (2002) *Children's Special Places: Exploring the Role of Forts, Dens and Bush Houses in Middle Childhood*. Detroit, MI: Wayne State University Press.

Striniste, N.A. and Moore, R.C. (1989) Early childhood outdoors: a literature review related to the design of childcare environments, *Children's Environments*, 6(4): 25–31.

Suransky, V.P. (1982) *The Erosion of Childhood*. Chicago: University of Chicago Press.

Titman, W. (1994) *Special Places; Special People: The Hidden Curriculum of School Grounds*. Godalming: World Wide Fund For Nature/Learning through Landscapes.

Topal, C.W. and Gandini, L. (1999) *Beautiful Stuff: Learning With Found Materials*. Worcester, MA: Davis Publications.

Tovey, H. (2007) *Playing Outdoors: Spaces and Places, Risk and Challenge*. Maidenhead: Open University Press.

White, J. (2010) *Toddlers Outdoors: Play, Learning and Development*. Newcastle: Siren Films.

White, J. (2011) *Two Year-Olds Outdoors: Play, Learning and Development*. Newcastle: Siren Films.

Woolley, H. and Lowe, A. (2013) Exploring the relationship between design approach and play value of outdoor play spaces, *Landscape Research*, 38(1): 53–74.

3   Exploring appropriate outdoor provision for babies and toddlers

Jan White

Introduction

> *Childhood has its own ways of seeing, thinking and feeling; nothing is more foolish than to try and substitute our ways.*
>
> *(Jean Jacques Rousseau)*

This chapter presents an exploration of what might be meant by outdoor play for the youngest children in the UK. I will discuss a range of developmental processes that are sustained by well-supported time in rich outdoor environments, and which have profound influences upon the wellbeing and development of babies and toddlers. In highlighting its significance in helping very young children to thrive and grow, I will make the case for the critical importance of being outdoors during the first two years of life.

With limited understanding of just how much nature and the outdoors can contribute to wellbeing and growth, feelings and attitudes about babies and very young children being outdoors may be moving towards a more negative position; however, this is a complex area, lacking a clear picture of parental and practitioner attitudes towards the outdoors for very young children. There is little evidence regarding how much children in this age group are actually outside in care and education settings, the nature of the outdoor environments they are accessing, and what they are able to experience and do once there. Informal research suggests that both time and range of experiences for babies and toddlers in group settings are highly limited (Carol Duffy, personal communication 2013).

Similarly, little formal research is available into what constitutes appropriate and effective provision outdoors for babies and toddlers. Decision-making regarding suitable outdoor environments and experiences for infants from birth to 2 therefore lacks evidential underpinnings. In practice there appears to be emphases upon the vulnerability of young children (where their competence and robustness is little recognized), risk aversion and avoidance, and several assumed dangers of the outdoors rather than its benefits; however, humans evolved outdoors over many millennia, and our bodies, minds and spirits need it: 'Human beings evolved outdoors. Our bodies need sunlight and fresh air. Our minds need the experiences and challenges that nature presents. Our souls need the day to day appreciation for the miracle of the world and all its complexity.' (Greenman 2007: 286).

This chapter presents literature that supports a more rational and theoretically rigorous basis for decision-making in this area. The process for exploring what might be appropriate and required experience outdoors for babies and toddlers presented here uses a developmental rationale to construct the overall case for *being* outdoors, and also to indicate some key conditions and experiences that should be offered through harnessing the special nature of the outdoors (White 2011). As an area in particular need of examination, this chapter focuses on outdoor provision for children from birth to 2. A similar analysis is needed to explore what might be appropriate provision for 2-year-olds, focusing on such aspects as the emergence of social play, imagination and language use. It should at all times be kept in mind that every child is supported to develop at their own rate and in their individual way.

In considering experiences for this age group, it is critical to bear in mind that adults and very young children inhabit substantially different worlds. Children live in a world of now, body, sensation, feeling and action, whereas adults dwell more in the world of mind, function, possibility and consequence. 'All these differences between children and adults suggest that children's consciousness, the texture of their everyday experience of the world, must be very different from ours. Children's brains and minds are radically different from ours, so their experience must be too.' (Gopnik 2009: 14). We exist in the same space, but perceive and experience it entirely differently. It is therefore necessary to investigate how the baby or toddler might be experiencing this place. What do they notice, what is their attention drawn to, what interests them? This kind of information indicates what is relevant for this child and what development might be going on in their mind and body (Gopnik et al. 1999). Such close looking helps us seek perspectives that will be very different from ours, and which are in turn crucial for working out what particular experiences the provision we make should be offering.

The sections that follow examine selected developmental experiences that illustrate the range and depth of impact of being outside during the first two years. The implications of these discussions raise themes and issues to critique and challenge current assumptions or discourses, and inform thinking about possible responses regarding provision and practice.

Exploring key experiences for babies and toddlers

> *Babies belong outside. Infants and toddlers deserve natural outdoor spaces that challenge their emerging sensory and physical skills and are* good places to be *for babies and to be* with *babies.*
>
> *(Greenman 2007: 300)*

Sensing and making sense of the world

Babies exist in a state of sensorial 'here-and-now', dominated by sensation and feeling. Awareness of separateness, past and future has yet to develop (Taylor 2009), thus sensory information from their surroundings feeds how they experience life. The outdoors is a wonderfully sensorial place for infants: consider for example the sensory texture of air and breeze, with the play of light and shadow, warmth and cold, moist and dry, smell and taste as it moves over the baby's skin, hair and tongue (White 2010a). Each sensory system is also developing rapidly during the earliest years in response to experience. As brain cortex 'wires up' for interpretation of sense-specific information, modulation (managing information so that it is not overwhelming) and integration (aligning sensory systems to give more complex interpretation) are also critical processes taking place (Kranowitz 2005). Making sense (meaning) of the world requires an environment where the quality of sensing (information) is rich.

Babies and toddlers must therefore have a richly multi-sensory environment that at the same time is not too overwhelming. Treasure baskets and heuristic play have been highly successful in supporting such provision (Gascoyne 2012), and this approach can be extended by enabling the child to discover what an outdoor environment filled with plants, water, natural materials, weather, seasons and people has to offer. That a nature-filled outdoor environment is able to provide such sensorial intensity without overwhelming is understood by the concepts of 'soft fascinations' and 'effortless attention' from attention restoration theory (Kaplan 1995) in that this is the environment in which we evolved, and are therefore most comfortable with. This theory is supported by recent research with mobile electroencephalography (EEG) where significant differences in adult brain-state between hard and soft outdoor environments were found (Aspinall et al. 2013). It will be interesting to see the results when neurological research is able to access young children's brain states in a similar way.

Developing vision and hearing

Being outdoors is particularly important for the complex development of vision, much of which takes place during the first year (Gopnik 2009). Focal range is extended, and at 3 months babies' attention seems to be drawn to high visual contrast (such as fences, walls, rooftops), at 5 months to moving objects and at 10 months to moving around objects (White 2010a). This attention may be building apparatus in the brain to manage complex visual information. Thus at first objects can be discerned from a background, then comprehended as stable things (understanding two-dimensional space), and finally seen as stable while perspective changes (understanding depth and three-dimensional space) (Gibson 1986; Hoffman 1998). A visually rich landscape providing objects ranging widely in size, things moving in different directions, light and shade, reflection and shadow, colours, shades and visual textures, and changing depth and perspectives (inside and outside, near to far, ground and sky) is necessary for the many elements of full visual development. All of these are naturally and readily available outdoors.

Hearing is likewise a highly complex system that is well supported outdoors. Indoors a relatively limited range of sounds is confused by reflection from the walls, easily becoming an unpleasant cacophony. The outdoor world is a soundscape of different, intriguing and 'clean' noises, where babies and toddlers can learn to attend to them (attention), pick out a particular sound (foregrounding), hear sounds separately and consider what is different between them (discrimination), work out what the sound relates to (remembering and association), locate the source, its distance and direction (localizing), track moving sounds (across and moving closer or further away), and sequence sounds (Kranowitz 2005). Hearing, vision and balance (see below) integrate during this time to provide a particularly powerful support system, especially once the child is able to move him- or herself in an audio-, visual- and physically-rich environment. The action of making sounds and moving itself are also known to stimulate vocalization, since movement of the body and use of the voice are neurologically linked (McGilchrist 2009). Thus children are more likely to use their own voice when being active outdoors.

Sleeping

> *Insufficient sleep may contribute to many contemporary childhood troubles. There is mounting evidence that . . . 'an epidemic of sleeplessness' is helping to fuel the rising incidence of behavioural and emotional problems among children.*
>
> *(Martin 2002)*

Sleeping is such a significant occupation for very young children that the quality of daytime sleep is an important consideration for childcare settings. Sleep is vital, nourishing and health promoting. As well as replenishing the brain, sleep provides the conditions for processing recent experiences and building the neural connections (memory) that enables the child to both make sense and make use of these experiences (Martin 2002). Given the amount and intensity of mental activity taking place when so much is new to them, it is not surprising that babies and toddlers need frequent bouts of rest and recovery within their day; however, it has also been shown that children in the UK generally do not get all of the sleep they need (Mental Health Foundation 2011). Babies need between 4 and 2.5 hours sleep during the day (at 6 months and 12 months respectively), and 2-year-olds should have around 1.5 hours naptime (NHS Choices 2013). The quality of sleep matters as much as the quantity, and children often settle better, sleep for longer, wake more gently and are more refreshed by having their naps outside in cool, oxygen-rich air – which is common practice in Scandinavia (Tourula et al. 2008). Some current practice would suggest that the change from outdoor daytime sleep to almost universally indoors in the UK over just one or two generations (BBC News Magazine 2013) is now beginning to reverse in early childhood care and education settings, and this would be greatly informed by research into its effectiveness.

Moving in space and gravity

Babies need to be rocked, finding this motion soothing and stimulating. Being moved through space – swinging, swooping, flying, hanging upside down, jiggling, dropping, bouncing and being swirled around are also delighted in, especially in body games with an adult with whom they feel completely safe. Such experiences give pronounced feelings of motion in space and provide sensations that develop vestibular organs in the inner ear, which tell us where we are in space in relation to the force of gravity. The vestibular sensory system underpins the development of brain organization, balance, body control and coordination, which themselves underpin a great deal else both physically and emotionally (Goddard Blythe 2004).

> Vestibular input seems to 'prime' the entire nervous system to function effectively. When the vestibular system does not function in a consistent and accurate way, the interpretations of other sensations will be inconsistent and inaccurate, and the nervous system will have trouble 'getting started'.
>
> (Ayres, cited in Kranowitz 2005: 115)

Having a strong sense of motion and balance gives a feeling of equilibrium and wellbeing, allowing us to feel comfortable in our body, to cope in the world and to feel confident in it. It is a vitally important developmental process that can only mature through movement of the body in space and gravity, requiring very many stimulatory movement experiences every day from before birth and into adolescence (Goddard Blythe 2004), and especially during the years from birth to 3. Finding space for swinging, bouncing, sliding, running, see-sawing, jumping off low walls and rolling down hills is important – as is engaging in plenty of body play with adults (DeBenedet and Cohen 2010).

Crawling, walking, moving and being active

Crawling is an exceptionally important stage in the first year of life, and should continue to be encouraged after walking develops. It trains the balance mechanism in a new relationship with gravity and helps to align the spine in preparation first for standing and then for walking. Crawling also opens up the hands. This kind of locomotion requires the use of all four limbs, combining left and right sides and upper and lower sections of the body in coordinated movement reflecting growing communication between the two hemispheres of the brain (Goddard Blythe 2008: 166).

Crawling babies need a variety of surfaces to provide different tactile experiences on which to develop movement skills. Crossing from one surface to another brings attention to contrasting sensations and a change in how they need to use their body. Paving is hard, cool, smooth and resistant; grass is warm, soft, firm and possibly wet, while sand is soft and yielding. Gravel is sharp and loose, but bark is warm, moist and graspable. Tarmac is hard and rough, while decking might be warm and ridged – and all will offer different smells! There is no indication that rubber matting should be more than just one of this rich mosaic of surfaces, that babies and toddlers need this to prevent injury, nor that it supports the development of walking. In light of the paucity of research in this area, it is likely that its dominance in outdoor spaces for this age group has developed from the current vulnerability and danger discourses previously mentioned, rather than starting from developmental value.

> Infants' everyday experiences with locomotion occur in truly massive doses . . . walking infants practice keeping balance in upright stance and locomotion for more than 6 accumulated hours per day. They average between 500 and 1,500 walking steps per hour so that by the end of each day, they may have taken 9,000 walking steps and travelled the length of 29 football fields.
>
> (Adolph et al. 2003: 494)

This immense drive for movement requires unhindered space, stimulus for moving, challenge for pushing abilities, permission and appropriate support from adults. It cannot be comfortably met indoors – and especially not in the containment devices such as pushchairs, car seats, baby bouncers and high chairs which are so common in current UK lifestyles. Such constraint results in babies and toddlers with pent-up movement needs that leave them frustrated, passive and severely underfed with the neurological stimulation they need. Children mastering balance and locomotion must have ample, daily opportunity to move in many different ways, and surfaces to move on that demand attention, effort, control and refined response beyond that which the uniform nature of indoor flooring requires. A variety of rich 'terrain' in the outdoor landscape can offer sloping, uneven and less predictable surfaces, non-resistant surfaces that 'give' underfoot, and a variety of levels with a range of ways of moving between them. The variability in an infant's walking experience may lie at the heart of developmental change. Thousands of walking steps, 'each step slightly different from the last because of variations in the terrain and the continuously varying biometric constraints on the body', facilitate mastery and flexibility in use of the body in new circumstances (Adolph et al. 2003).

Given the significance of these stages for foundational developments that influence the rest of the child's life, it is clearly important to consider how they can be supported outdoors all through the year, how being outdoors enhances the experience, and how to harness the special nature of the outdoors to add depth, range and challenge to the experience. Motor control and coordination are so important for life functioning that we must recognize that these active, robust and competent explorers are more than capable of coping with such challenge. A desert of tarmac, concrete paving or rubber surfacing is developmentally inadequate for children of this age. 'It doesn't help a child to tackle a difficult task if they succeed constantly on an easy one. It doesn't teach them to persist in the face of obstacles if obstacles are always eliminated.' (Dweck, cited in Claxton 1999: 35).

Concern by the medical profession about the increasingly sedentary nature of young children's lives has led to official recommendations for children from birth to 5 (Department of Health 2011) of a minimum of three hours of activity a day. Practitioners should give serious consideration to how active each of the children are, in what ways the routines and practices of the setting unnecessarily restrict how much children are active, and how they can stimulate and enable children to be more active. Provocations and resources that encourage movement and activity, walks into the locality just outside the setting, active adults who engage in physical play with infants, and work with parents on this issue, are all possible avenues for increasing activity levels and reducing sedentary behaviour.

Exploring natural elements

Young children are endlessly interested in and biologically programmed to explore the stuff of the earth, how materials behave and what they do (Kellert 1993). Because of the central role of earth and water in the workings of the world, it is not really surprising that children are so drawn to them and find so much that is fascinating to do with them. If young children are to make meaning of their world, they must have abundant time and opportunity to play actively with its basic elements. Soil, sand, plants, water and puddles are truly intriguing things when young children interact with them. Young children need extensive experience of such materials under naturally changing conditions outside, as well as copious opportunities to investigate wetness and *being* wet.

New understandings about the role of environmental germs in building a well-functioning immune system, and the prevention of allergy development, indicate that 'dirt is good for you' and that children actually benefit from exposure to soil and other sources of beneficial bacteria (National Wildlife Federation 2012). Research suggests that contact with earth also helps the body to make serotonin, a neurotransmitter that makes us feel happy and capable, via the common soil bacteria *Mycobacterium vaccae* (Lowry et al. 2007). The medically supported 'hygiene hypothesis' suggests that being exposed to the benign germs with which we have evolved is important for our health, and that harm is done by over-sanitizing children (Ruebush 2009). Such growing understandings suggest that it is necessary to reassess assumptions about the vulnerability of young children and the desirability of eradication of all germs. Our aim should be to seek a reasonable, proportionate and healthy balance.

Making things happen

> *The thirst for understanding springs from the child's deepest emotional needs . . . [it is] a veritable passion.*
>
> (Isaacs 1932)

As babies interact with their environment they pay particular attention to how events link together (cause and effect), how one thing leads to another (causation) and gradually come to realize that they themselves can make things happen. Exploring cause and effect is an enormously important cognitive and affective process occupying much of the lives of older babies and toddlers, especially outdoors (White 2010a and b). Repeated experience of linking events leads to theory building (working models that help in meaning making, Carr and Lee 2012) and the construction of neural networks that result in new thinking abilities. This is especially effective when the child is the one making things happen since they experience simultaneous internal and external feedback from the event, providing multi-sensory information for interpretive processing. The prevalence of schematic enquiries at a sensory-motor level at this age is a manifestation of this process (Atherton and Nutbrown 2013). The greater the amount of sensory information being fed into the child's body, especially internally through the motion-detecting vestibular sense and the body-awareness sense of proprioception (Kranowitz 2005), the more they are able to think about the experience – we think in all the ways we experience (Robinson 2009). Being able to push, pull, carry, manipulate and transport large, heavy and awkward items in the larger space of outdoor environments is therefore particularly valuable.

Linking up what it feels like in their body with what they detect from the outside world helps a child to determine what they have caused rather than what simply happens. Realizing personal causality helps to distinguish 'self' from the external world, developing self-awareness and identity (Fernyhough 2008: 67). Moving from 'what does this do?' to 'what can *I* make it do?', the baby or toddler can experience the pleasurable and powerful feelings that *they* can make things happen, contributing to the growth of agency, a key part of mental wellbeing (Roberts 2010). Repeated direct experience of cause and effect gradually allows the child to imagine, or predict, what will happen next time. Imagining the future is the basis of creativity. Thus understanding causation is necessary for the development of the imagination and being able to think about what might be as well as what is (Gopnik 2009). An outdoor environment that presents a wide range of cause and effect experiences will be a powerfully enabling environment for babies and toddlers.

Being together with adults

The very young child's comfort in the outdoors rests on experiencing it with an emotionally attached adult (Robinson 2003). The close presence of an attentive, attuned adult is critical to allow the child to feel safe, secure and 'held', so providing the safe base that enables them to focus outward to explore their environment. Such 'holding' allows a child to gain familiarity and confidence in this environment, so that they can explore further into the affordances it has for them.

Increasing independence to explore and investigate only comes from knowing that this adult, while not necessarily directly interacting, is nearby, attentive and available. Driven by a strong survival instinct, the toddler needs to check this frequently and receive rapid reassurance (Gerhardt 2004). Interesting new research (Singer et al. 2013) revealed that the level of involvement in activity (Lavers 1994) by preschool children when adults were seated and stationary in the classroom were higher than when they roamed around the indoor environment. The more quickly children could locate the adult to feel secure, the more readily they were able to resume their play. Plenty of well-placed and comfortable seating outdoors can support adults in providing the safe base that toddlers moving away from adults need, and also ensure that adults can respond to the rapid changes in energy levels of babies and toddlers, providing comfort and recovery after activity, offer a lap from which young children can watch others, or simply enjoy companionship while taking pleasure in being outdoors together.

Babies and toddlers are best moved around in adult arms, held in adults' laps, laid on the ground, or free to be mobile. As companionable learners (Roberts 2011), being alongside and thinking together, adults can harness the strategy of 'slowliness' (Sightlines Initiative 2008) to focus on the rich detail of the child's pace and agenda, and use companionable conversations (Dowling 2013) to naturally support language and thinking.

Key themes, issues and opportunities

The area of appropriate and effective outdoor provision for babies and toddlers is in great need of attention and research. In this section I identify some key themes, issues and opportunities relating to the development of access and experiences outdoors for children from birth to 2. These relate to acknowledgement of the value of being outdoors, the importance of adult attitudes and practice, changes required in policy, and the need for further research.

Acknowledging the uniqueness and value of the outdoors:

- The outdoors is different from indoors and has its own special nature. It is this that must be focused upon in provision and practice (White 2011).

- Practitioners must take pleasure in being outside with very young children, be able to use the outdoors well and make the most of it, such as by noticing everyday nature. This has implications for initial training in particular, as well as ongoing CPD.

The importance of adult attitudes, actions and practice:

- Adults are the gate keepers for very young children's access to the outdoors, deciding when children go outdoors, how much time they have there, what potential experiences are available there and what they are permitted to actually do there. It is therefore critical that parents, providers and practitioners believe that this is a good place for a child to be, and necessary for wellbeing, learning and development.
- Good partnership working must be in place to reveal how parents feel about their child being outdoors, and to help them realize the benefits in their child accessing the full richness of the outdoors.
- Babies and toddlers need adults who have a conception of them as active learners capable of enduring the bumps and spills of childhood (Greenman 2007: 300) and who employ a 'benefit–risk approach' (Ball et al. 2008) to the provision and management of experiences.
- The outdoor environment must also meet the needs of practitioners so that they feel secure, supported, comfortable and confident, and so that they can therefore be calm, slow, attentive, attuned and available. If adults do not enjoy being outside, children will inevitably not spend long outdoors.

Changes to policy:

- An analysis of the visibility and discourses around the outdoors within the UK early years curricula and guidance for this age group (where they exist) would be valuable, with recommendations for strengthening attitudes and provision/practice. The relative lack of coverage of outdoors in recent practitioner texts for this age group is also of concern.

The need for further research:

- A great deal of research is needed, particularly to investigate the current situation, explore the attitudes held by parents, practitioners and leaders, and examine what makes outdoor environments rich and effective for babies and toddlers.
- Finding out how very young children experience their world and seeking the perspectives of this age group is challenging but vital. Although applied to the outdoors for children as young as 2½ years, the Mosaic approach (Clark and Moss 2005; Pinder 2005) has not yet

been examined as a method for this age group and may require the development of further techniques.

- Research into cultural and societal influences is also needed to bring to the surface assumptions and discourses driving current approaches to outdoor experiences for this age group, particularly the vulnerability of very young children over their competence and the danger of outdoors over its value. Our multi-cultural society may hold many different viewpoints and assumptions about, for example, the weather, health, risk and play versus learning.

Young children *must* be outdoors because it is integral to their physical, psychological and social development. Extensive and high quality experiences in the outdoors during the years from birth to 2 should be considered as a right and a requirement in all educative settings, and actively supported in home and family contexts.

The starting point for exploring appropriate outdoor provision is a careful consideration of what children need and want to be doing at each point in their lives from birth onwards, so as to derive the experiences they need to be having. This then leads on to rational, balanced and child-focused thinking about how to respond with provision and practice. It is our responsibility to give children the outdoor environments and experiences that they should have, and to work out how to do so within (or by overcoming) the constraints and limitations of our own situation.

References

Adolph, K., Vereijken, B. and Shrout, P. (2003) What changes in infant walking and why, *Child Development*, 74(2): 475–97.

Aspinall, P., Mavros, P., Coyne, R. and Roe, J. (2013) The urban brain: analysing outdoor physical activity with mobile EEG, *British Journal of Sports Medicine* Mar 6 [advance epub accessed 28.5.13 from www.ncbi.nim.nih.gov/pubmed/23467965].

Atherton, F. and Nutbrown, C. (2013) *Understanding Schemas and Young Children from Birth to Three*. London: Sage Publications Ltd.

Ball, D., Gill, T. and Spiegal, B. (2008) *Managing Risk in Play Provision: Implementation Guide*. London: Play England.

BBC News Magazine (2013) *Napping in a Hutch and Other Tales of Outdoor Snoozing*. www.bbc.co.uk/news/magazine-21575562 28 February 2013 (accessed 31 May 2013).

Carr, M. and Lee, W. (2012) *Learning Stories: Constructing Learner Identities in Early Education*. London: Sage Publications Ltd.

Clark, A. and Moss, P. (2005) *Spaces to Play: More Listening to Young Children Using the Mosaic Approach*. London: National Children's Bureau.

Claxton, G. (1999) *Wise up: Learning to Live the Learning Life*. Stafford: Network Educational Press Ltd.

DeBenedet, A.T. and Cohen, L.J. (2010) *The Art of Roughhousing: Good Old-Fashioned Horseplay and Why Every Kid Needs It*. Philadelphia, PA: Quirk Books.

Department of Health (2011) *Start Active, Stay Active: A Report on Physical Activity for Health from the Four Home Countries' Chief Medical Officers*. Downloadable from www.gov.uk/government/publications

Dowling, M. (2013) *Young Children's Thinking*. London: Sage Publications Ltd.

Fernyhough, C. (2008) *The Baby in the Mirror: A Child's World from Birth to Three*. London: Granta Books.

Gascoyne, S. (2012) *Treasure Baskets and Beyond: Realising the Potential of Sensory-rich Play*. Maidenhead: Open University Press.

Gerhardt, S. (2004) *Why Love Matters: How Affection Shapes a Baby's Brain*. Hove: Brunner-Routledge.

Gibson, J.J. (1986) *The Ecological Approach to Visual Perception*. Hove: Psychology Press.

Goddard Blythe, S. (2004) *The Well Balanced Child: Movement and Early Learning*. Stroud: Hawthorne Press.

Goddard Blythe, S. (2008) *What Babies and Children Really Need*. Stroud: Hawthorne Press.

Gopnik, A. (2009) *The Philosophical Baby: What children's Minds Tell Us About Truth, Love and the Meaning of Life*. London: The Bodley Head.

Gopnik, A., Meltzoff, A. and Kuhl, P. (1999) *How Babies Think: The Science of Childhood*. London: Weidenfield & Nicolson.

Greenman, J. (2007) *Caring Spaces, Learning Places: Children's Environments that Work*. Redmond: Exchange Press Inc.

Hoffman, D.D. (1998) *Visual Intelligence: How We Create What We See*. London: W.W. Norton & Company Inc.

Isaacs, S. (1932) *The Children We Teach*. London: University of London Press.

Kaplan, S. (1995) The restorative benefits of nature: towards an integrative framework, *Journal of Environmental Psychology*, 15: 169–82.

Kellert, S.R. (1993) The biological basis for human values of nature. In S.R. Kellert and E.O. Wilson (eds) *The Biophilia Hypothesis*. Washington, DC: Island Press.

Kranowitz, C.S. (2005) *The Out-of-Sync Child: Recognising and Coping with Sensory Processing Disorder*. London: Perigee Penguin Books.

Lavers, F. (ed.) (1994) *Defining and Assessing Quality in Early Childhood Education*. Leuven: Leuven University Press.

Lowry, C., Hollis, J.H., de Vries, A. et al. (2007) Identification of an immune-responsive mesolimbocortical serotonergic system: potential role in regulation of emotional behavior, *Neuroscience*, doi:10.1016/J.Neuroscience 2007.01.067

Martin, P. (2002) *Counting Sheep: The Science and Pleasures of Sleep and Dreams*. London: HarperCollins Publishers.

McGilchrist, I. (2009) *The Master and his Emissary: The Divided Brain and Making of the Western World*. London: Yale University Press.

Mental Health Foundation (2011) *Sleep Matters: The Impact of Sleep on Health and Wellbeing*. London: Mental Health Foundation. www.mentalhealth.org/publications/sleep-report (accessed 6 January 2013).

National Wildlife Federation (2012) *The Dirt on Dirt: How Getting Dirty Outdoors Benefits Kids*. http://www.nwf.org/Be-Out-There/Why-Be-Out-There/Dirt-is-Great.aspx (accessed 6 January 2013).

NHS Choices (2013) *How Much Sleep Do Kids Need?* www.nhs.uk/livewell/childrenssleep/pages/howmuchsleep.aspx (accessed 6 January 2013).

Pinder, C. (2005) *The Great Outdoors: Children's Lived Experiences at Walkergate Early Years Centre*. London: The Children's Society.

Roberts, R. (2010) *Wellbeing From Birth*. London: Sage Publications Ltd.

Roberts, R. (2011) Companiable learning: a mechanism for holistic well-being development from birth, *European Early Childhood Education Research Journal*, 19(2): 195–205.

Robinson, M. (2003) *From birth to one:* The year of opportunity. Buckingham: Open University Press.

Ruebush, M. (2009) *Why Dirt is Good: 5 Ways to Make Germs Your Friends*. New York: Kaplan Publishing.

Sightlines Initiative (2008) *Doing the Right Thing: Working with Children in a Natural Environment, Early Childhood Educators Revaluate their Theory and Practice*. Newcastle: Sightlines Initiative.

Singer, E., Nederend, M., Penninx, L., Tajik, M. and Boom, J. (2013) *The teacher's role in supporting young children's level of play engagement*. Paper presented at EECERA conference, Tallinn, 28–31 August.

Taylor, J.B. (2009) *My Stroke of Insight: A Brain Scientist's Personal Journey*. London: Hodder & Stoughton Ltd.

Tourula, M., Isola, A. and Hassi, J. (2008) Children sleeping outdoors in winter: parents' experiences of a culturally bound childcare practice, *International Journal of Circumpolar Health*, 67(2–3): 269–78.

White, J. (2010a) *Babies Outdoors: Play, Learning and Development*. Newcastle: Siren Films Ltd.

White, J. (2010b) *Toddlers Outdoors: Play, Learning and Development*. Newcastle: Siren Films Ltd.

White, J. (2011) Capturing the Difference: The Special Nature of the Outdoors. In J. White (ed.) *Outdoor Provision in the Early Years*. London: Sage Publications Ltd.

Section 2

Policy and practice in the UK

4 Supporting 'child-initiated' activity in the outdoor environment

Trisha Maynard

Introduction

In the mid-1990s, following the introduction of the National Curriculum and assessment system, I was involved in a project in which five early years teachers in Wales were asked to mentor an aspect of subject knowledge to student teachers on placement in their schools. Initially these teachers objected strongly to this; describing themselves as 'child centred' they dismissed the importance of subject knowledge for themselves as teachers and for the children in their classes. They also made clear their irritation that the amount of prescribed content in the National Curriculum forced them to teach superficially, focusing on 'subjects' rather than on children's emotional and social development and their positive attitudes towards learning through relevant and meaningful experiences (see Maynard 1996).

Less than a decade later, following devolution in 1999, the Welsh Government expressed concern about the overly formal curriculum and approaches to teaching adopted within some early years and Key Stage 1 classes in Wales. Proposals were published for a new curriculum framework for children aged 3 to 7 years – so replacing Key Stage 1 of the National Curriculum – which maintained the centrality of children's wellbeing and personal and social development and promoted active, play-based experiential learning, the inclusion of child-initiated activity and greater use of the outdoor environment (NAfW 2003).

This, the swing between the apparently opposing discourses of child-centred and subject-centred education, provides the policy backdrop for this chapter. The main focus, however, is on 'child-initiated' activity (play and learning) in the outdoor environments of early years classes. In this chapter I argue that:

- 'child-initiated' activity has many benefits for young children;
- supporting 'child-initiated' activity is challenging and requires the development of complex cognitive skills, including the ability to loosen control;

- the outdoor environment provides a particularly appropriate and supportive context for 'child-initiated' activity – both for children and
  teachers;
- 'child-initiated' activity may be associated with child-centred
  approaches but it still requires teachers to have secure subject knowledge so as to support children's later understandings of key ideas and
  processes.

First, however, I turn to a brief consideration of the policy backdrop.

Child-centred education

The western tradition of early years education, dating back to early years
pioneers such as Friedrich Froebel, has a long and strong association with
child-centred approaches. Such approaches resonate with a view of childhood as 'joyful and carefree' (Pramling Samuelsson and Johansson 2006: 48)
and see the child as intrinsically curious and capable (Kwon 2002). Free play
is seen as important as is first-hand learning which stems from individual
children's interests and cuts across subject boundaries; this is supported by
the teacher acting as guide and facilitator rather than instructor (Kwon 2002).
Learning in and through nature has also been seen as a key element of this
approach, and in the UK, from the beginning of the twentieth century, particular emphasis was placed on the nursery garden as a stimulating, real-life environment in which children were given the space and time to play and explore
(Bilton 2010).

Child-centred approaches appeared to gain official status in the publication of the Hadow Report (Hadow 1931). Paradoxically this was around the
time at which the centrality of the nursery garden, and with it the amount of
outdoor play, began to decline (Bilton 2010); however, it is most strongly associated with the Plowden Report (CACE 1967) which maintained, for example,
that 'At the heart of the educational process lies the child' (para 9) and that 'A
teacher who relies only on instruction, who forestalls children's questions or
who answers them too quickly, instead of asking further questions which will
set children on their way to their own solution, will disincline children to learn'
(para 531).

It is questionable how far child-centred approaches were actually imple-
mented in primary classrooms at this time but such approaches were exten-
sively critiqued – particularly by those from the New Right who maintained
that it was the teacher's duty to direct: to 'pass on skills and wisdom to children,
and to ensure that they are trained in civilized manners and ways of thought'
(Cox and Dyson 1971: 21). O'Hear (1991) stated that there was no reason why
children from the age of 5 shouldn't engage in rote learning and be taught
mathematical tables and phonics while Chris Woodhead, as Chief Inspector of

Schools, later argued that even teachers of 3- and 4- year-old children should employ formal, direct teaching methods (Woodhead 1999 in Kwon 2002).

Concerns about child-centred approaches were reflected in the establishment of a National Curriculum and assessment system for children of 5–16 years (Education Reform Act of 1988). This initiative set out to raise standards within a global marketplace (Soler and Miller 2003) through putting 'subjects' rather than the 'child' at the centre of the curriculum (Alexander et al. 1992). Thus the teacher was reframed as an 'instructor' rather than 'facilitator' while an emphasis was placed on whole class teaching rather than individual activity. In 1996 the National Curriculum was followed in England and Wales by the introduction of the first curriculum framework for children under 5 – *Desirable Outcomes for Children's Learning on Entering Compulsory Education* (SCAA 1996).

The situation in Wales

In Wales, following devolution in 1999, there was a desire to identify and implement education policies that were both effective and relevant to Wales (NAfW 2001): it was noted that 'we share key strategic goals with England – but we often need to take a different route to achieve them' (NAfW 2001: 2). Thus while as in England there was also a concern to meet the challenges of the globalized marketplace and raise standards of literacy and numeracy, it was felt that this should not be through the use of 'overly-formal' approaches to teaching and learning in the first few years of school. Such approaches, it was maintained, are 'developmentally inappropriate' and also do not support the development of children as lifelong learners (NAfW 2003). It was noted that in Scandinavian countries there is little or no formal teaching of literacy and numeracy until the children are older and as a result, 'when children in these countries are introduced to the more formal literacy skills, they make rapid progress' (p. 11).

Building on the republished 'Desirable Outcomes' (ACCAC 2000), the Foundation Phase Framework thus advocates an experiential, play-based approach to learning for children aged 3 to 7 years. The Framework broadly resonates with child-centred ideas stating that the child should be at the heart of any planned curriculum and maintaining the centrality of children's wellbeing and their personal and social development (DCELLS 2008a). It advocates the inclusion of child-initiated activities while an emphasis is placed on learning in the outdoor environment with children being given opportunities to 'take risks' and 'become confident explorers' (DCELLS 2008a: 16).

However, the Framework also identifies a clear role for the adult in supporting, guiding and extending children's thinking and learning and incorporates teacher-directed activities. Further, while the Foundation Phase is structured around seven 'areas of learning' (rather than subjects) it retains a statutory, detailed, skills-focused curriculum with outcomes cross-referenced to National Curriculum level descriptors (see Maynard et al. 2013a).

What, then, are the benefits of child-initiated play and learning?

Child-initiated play and learning

Child-initiated activity is closely associated with children's spontaneous, free or self-chosen play or investigation (Lindon 2013): that is, experiences that are both initiated and led by the child. It has been argued that play – free play – has the potential to support children's learning and development across the curriculum (Bruce 2011) and has been linked to wider benefits including children's physical and mental health, emotional wellbeing, creativity and social inclusion as well as positive dispositions (Wood 2010a). Indeed, Wood (2010b) notes that some of the qualities and characteristics of such play include attentiveness, curiosity, resilience, responsiveness, openness and flexibility: as noted below, such dispositions are also seen as significant for supporting children's development as learners (Claxton and Carr 2004).

A view of the child as a naturally curious and competent learner has much in common with the philosophy adopted by the infant and toddler centres of the municipality of Reggio Emilia in Italy. According to this philosophy children are active participants in their own socialization and knowledge building (Rinaldi 1998). They are viewed as 'rich in potential, strong, powerful and competent' (Malaguzzi 1993: 10) and as connected to other members of the community; it is an educational system based on relationships (Malaguzzi 1993). Children and teachers form 'a partnership of learning' (Gandini 1993: 6) and young children seek to make sense of their worlds through interactions and collaborations and through symbolically representing and testing out their ideas using different media. As noted in Maynard and Chicken (2010) there is no predetermined curriculum; rather, Reggio pedagogues make use of organic projects in which there is an emphasis on obtaining group understanding through constant dialogue, a dialogue driven on by different and often conflicting viewpoints. Through group analysis of dialogue, observations and annotated representations (documentation) there is an attempt to make visible children's learning and understand their emergent theories.

Valuing the child as a competent learner has clear implications for practice; Claxton and Carr (2004) refer to the need to support children's positive learning dispositions – an individual's characteristic way of responding to the environment. Dispositions such as confidence, curiosity, resilience, playfulness and so on can be strengthened or weakened depending on teachers' actions and interactions when working with children. Importantly, Claxton and Carr (2004) refer to 'potentiating' (powerful) environments in which positive dispositions are actively stretched and developed through shared experiences in which children as well as adults take responsibility for directing activities.

The importance of fostering positive dispositions resonates with Deci and Ryan's (2002) theory of 'self determination' which points to the significance of supporting feelings of 'competence', 'relatedness' and 'autonomy' if individuals are to reach their potential: that is, feeling effective and being given opportunities to demonstrate this; feeling connected to others; feeling in control of one's life and comfortable with one's behaviour. Similarly, Dweck's (2000) work demonstrates that supporting children's intrinsic motivation is vital if children are to develop a 'mastery orientation' towards learning as opposed to 'learned helplessness'. Intrinsic motivation is also associated with supporting creative thinking: 'thinking that is novel and that produces ideas that are of value' (Sternberg 2003: 325–6). In their research, Robson and Rowe (2012) found that the most frequently occurring aspects of creative thinking (trying out ideas, analysing ideas and involving others) were strongly associated with child-initiated activity (see also Craft et al. 2008).

Our projects

The next part of the chapter draws on the findings of the three projects which, inspired by the philosophy of the preschools of Reggio Emilia, explored 'child-initiated' play and learning with groups of Foundation Phase teachers. The three projects formed part of a series of five studies that followed the staging of the Reggio Emilia Travelling Exhibition at Swansea University. The projects each involved seven or eight early years teachers chosen by the funders: two local authorities in South Wales. The first project (Maynard and Chicken 2010) asked children to initiate Reggio-inspired projects within their classrooms (although some did go outdoors); the second (Maynard et al. 2011) aimed to investigate whether teachers' practice differed when supporting these projects in the outdoor environment. In both of these studies it was noted that 'child-initiated' learning and/or the outdoor environment appeared to have a positive effect on children who were seen as 'underachieving' in the classroom setting. The third project (Maynard et al. 2013b) intended to explore this issue in more depth, to find out whether 'child-initiated' learning outdoors did have any effect on these children and if so, the extent, nature and possible reasons for this.

While the projects had different foci they broadly followed a similar format: the teachers attended university-based seminars or workshops focused on a consideration of relevant theories, ideas and research methods and undertook a series of related tasks in their classes. In the second half of each study, the teachers also engaged in supporting 'child-initiated' play and learning (Reggio-inspired projects) within the indoor and outdoor environments of their settings. Details of the methods and analysis are not possible in this short chapter but can be found in the relevant papers.

It is important to note, however, that within the Foundation Phase documentation 'child-initiated activities' – that is, children's spontaneous and free play – are differentiated from 'practitioner-initiated activities' ('structured educational play'; DCELLS 2008b: 5) which may be child-led or practitioner-led (see Maynard et al. 2013a). Although 'structured educational play' should have specific, planned outcomes for children's learning, it is maintained that children should not be made to pursue a particular activity (DCELLS 2008c) or discouraged from developing their own ideas (DCELLS 2008b). When supporting 'structured educational play', then, sensitivity to the child's ideas and interests are also paramount. That is, while providing for meaningful activity teachers should work alongside children not only as facilitator or play partner but also as co-constructor or guide and through their sensitive actions and interactions help children to make visible their current theories and consider these in relation to new (and potentially subject-related) ideas.

Within our projects we broadly characterized 'child-initiated' activities as those: that were both initiated and led by the child, which did not have predetermined (subject content) outcomes; in which the activity centred on play or self-chosen investigation; which involved open interaction; and in which the teacher acted as facilitator or co-researcher (see Maynard et al. 2011). However, it became apparent that whether working indoors or out, most teachers did not (or could not) allow children to initiate activities; in Maynard et al. (2011) we note that 87 per cent of observed activities were practitioner-initiated. This being the case, in this chapter I use the term 'child-initiated' (in single inverted commas) to refer to activities where the control either lies in the hands of the child or is shared between child and adult: activities that, in Claxton and Carr's (2004) terms, can form part of a 'potentiating' environment. In this way it incorporates some activities more accurately categorized as 'structured educational play'.

What then, were our key findings?

The key findings

At the beginning of the first project (Maynard and Chicken 2010), while teachers maintained their commitment to child-centred values, they recognized that their activities and pedagogy were not entirely consistent with these. For example, when the teachers first introduced project work, most devised an initial stimulus activity that was used to guide children towards finding out factual information: for example, 'What do you want to know about minibeasts?' While the teachers provided children with greater choice, this was normally a choice between several content-focused activities. The teachers reported that after a while their projects floundered – one teacher suggested that this was because they were too linear and content focused. Eventually some teachers allowed children to contribute to the direction in which activities developed and made greater use of open questioning; however, spending time listening to children and supporting or extending their emergent ideas and theories was found to be extremely challenging.

Analysis of video-data from the second project (Maynard et al. 2011) revealed a number of differences (some statistically significant) between the teachers' normal classroom practice and their practice when supporting Reggio-inspired projects in the outdoor environment. For example, it was found that when supporting 'child-initiated' play and learning outdoors teachers were:

- more likely in their planning to include broader (non-content) out-comes such as social skills;
- more likely to allow children to lead activities (either wholly or in part);
- more likely to allow children to engage in 'free and structured play';
- more likely to take on the role of facilitator/support or adopt a 'mixed' pedagogical approach;
- more likely to use open questions;
- more likely to include activities with a higher level of cognitive challenge, physical challenge (risk-taking) and physical activity.

As we recognized (Maynard et al. 2011), involvement in this project, and the focus on 'child-initiated' learning, is likely to have accounted for some of these observed differences; similar although more subtle differences were noticed in the first study when teachers supported 'child-initiated' learning in their class-rooms. We concluded, however, that they were also related in some way to the environment in which these activities took place; we noted, for example, that even before the teachers began to introduce Reggio-inspired projects there was a difference between their practice and the children's behaviour when indoors and out.

In the third project (Maynard et al. 2013b) we were interested in exploring teachers' assertions in the previous two projects that 'child-initiated' activity – particularly when undertaken outdoors – had a particular effect on children whom their teachers' perceived to be 'underachieving': that is who were seen to be experiencing either social or emotional difficulties or who were struggling with the literacy or numeracy. This study found that in the case studies of over half of the 48 target children, the teachers reported that they had observed positive differences when children were engaged in Reggio-inspired projects outdoors. For example, these children were perceived to demonstrate greater concentration, engagement and enjoyment and an increased willingness to help others and share ideas.

Supporting 'child-initiated' activity

So what was it about the outdoor environment that supported – and appeared to enable teachers better to support – 'child-initiated' activity? Here I refer to three inter-related aspects: 'features', 'the affordance of space' and 'associations'.

Features

As researchers have noted, the natural outdoor environment provides a rich, sensory context for children's play and investigations (Fjørtoft 2004; Waite et al. 2006). When outdoors children can explore the world at first hand and *experience* natural phenomena such as the weather, changing seasons and shadows (Ouvry 2003). In our studies, the outdoor spaces in which most activities took place were rich in 'loose parts' such as stones, twigs and sticks so supporting children's play, exploration and creativity (see Nicholson 1971). Trawick-Smith (1994) notes the need for children to negotiate the meaning of loose parts within their play; this may encourage children to initiate interactions with their peers and so support a sense of 'relatedness'. An abundance of loose parts outdoors has also been found to stimulate children in initiating conversations with their teachers (Waters and Maynard 2010).

The ever-changing natural environment may also enhance children's sense of wellbeing. In our second project (Maynard et al. 2011) the teachers reported that when outdoors the children appeared happier and that the outdoor environment seemed to calm some children and excite others; Stephenson notes that increased levels of stimulation and emotional and spiritual wellbeing have been attributed to the 'variations in temperature, light, movement, colour, smell, texture' (Stephenson 2002: 31) experienced in the ever-changing outdoor space.

Researchers (for example, Kaplan 1995; Wells and Evans 2003) have maintained that 'green' outdoor environments can have a calming and restorative effect. Indeed, Kuo and Taylor (2004) note that exposure to such environments may be beneficial in reducing the symptoms of attention deficit hyperactivity disorder. In natural outdoor environments children may also have the opportunity to identify what have been called 'special places' (Sobel 1993) or 'secret places' (Moser and Martinsen 2010): small areas hidden from staff in which children can be on their own or with one or two others, sit quietly and reflect and recuperate before engaging in further play. Such places, according to Moser and Martinsen (2010), may be necessary for children's mental health and wellbeing. This seems to resonate with the teachers' assertions (Maynard and Chicken 2010; Maynard et al. 2011) that 'child-initiated' learning and/or the outdoor environment appeared to have a positive effect on children who were perceived to be 'underachieving' in the classroom: shy children became more confident, those who were boisterous or aggressive became calmer, more focused and better behaved.

Play in natural outdoor environments may also satisfy children's innate need for challenge and excitement (Bilton 2010; Little and Eager 2010). For example, researchers have noted that the features of the outdoor environment support the development of children's physical risk-taking behaviours (Sandseter 2007, 2009; Tovey 2007; Waters and Begley 2007) so contributing to the development of self-confidence (Santer et al. 2007) as well as to positive dispositions to learning such as resilience and reciprocity (Ouvry 2003).

The affordance of space

The space normally provided by the natural outdoor environment allows children to construct on a bigger scale and move around freely (Rivkin 1995) so suggesting particular types of activities that are arguably more meaningful to young children and which may promote and support, amongst others, children's sense of 'self-determination' (Deci and Ryan 2002). In our studies most project activities undertaken outdoors tended to focus on problem solving (creative thinking) and the use of gross motor skills (see Maynard et al. 2013b); we note that this was in contrast to the more formal and subject-centred activities undertaken in the classroom (such as formal literacy tasks) that were tightly controlled and often demanded the use of fine motor skills. What was referred to as the 'masking effect' of outdoor activities was also noted in relation to the behaviour of certain children; when engaged in 'child-initiated' activity children did not have to wait to take their turn as they did when part of larger group activities. This, and the space to get away from confrontation and conflict (Ouvry 2003), may have made children less likely to feel and demonstrate frustration.

Associations

Tuan (1977) maintains that in the western world 'space' signifies a sense of freedom and the opening up of possibilities. For the children, the outdoor environment may be perceived as free from adult control (Lester and Maudsley 2007) and therefore more open to the assertion of their agency and also to the possibilities of play (Lester and Maudsley 2007). As McInness et al. (2011) note, outdoor environments tend to be associated with fun and 'not work'. These associations may be related to the position of the outdoor environments relative to the school building; as Stephenson (2002) maintains, when outdoors children are away from the ordered, stable classroom that is dominated by rules and routines and almost in touching distance of the chaotic, real world. Particularly for those children in our projects who were struggling with their learning in the classroom, then, it may be that outdoor environments were not cluttered by negative emotions associated with feelings of underachievement (Maynard et al. 2013b).

In a previous study (Maynard 2007) I have suggested that classrooms were also seen as places of authority and control by the teachers and that their professional identities appeared almost to be embedded within the school walls. When outside, then, teachers may be less under the control of the dominant discourse of subjects and outcomes and in an environment that speaks more of traditional child-centred approaches. Certainly, the teachers in our second study (Maynard et al. 2011) reported that when outdoors they felt less pressurized and more relaxed, less of an authority figure and less constrained by targets and outcomes; similarly in our third study (Maynard et al. 2013b) a teacher commented that outside she felt 'less scrutinized'. These teachers (as also noted by Stephenson 2002) recognized that when outdoors they had different expectations of children; children were allowed to run around, make a mess and shout with excitement. This would not be tolerated in the classroom.

Thus, through its 'features', 'the affordance of space' and its 'associations', the outdoor environment provided a rich context for, and for helping teachers to support, 'child-initiated' learning.

Resistance

It is important to note that not all of the children involved in our studies enjoyed going outside or undertaking project activities. For example, in Maynard and Chicken (2010) we report that some children seen to be 'high achievers' – who wanted, and were used to, getting the right answer – found it difficult to take risks and devise solutions for the more complex and messy conceptual problems they encountered. Nor did all the teachers in our projects welcome this opportunity. For example, even when speaking nostalgically of a childhood spent outdoors, and noting the benefits of outdoor play, many appeared reluctant to take the children outside on a regular basis. These teachers often referred to a range of practical, structural and cultural constraints which prevented them from going outdoors such as inclement weather, difficulties with supervision and accessibility, vandalism and safety; however, we found that such concerns were not closely related to what teachers did; that is, while referring to these constraints, a small number of teachers still took the children outside (Maynard et al. 2011).

Rather, data from these studies illustrates that supporting 'child-initiated' play and learning in the outdoor environment presents significant challenges for teachers; it requires the development of complex cognitive skills (Maynard and Chicken 2010). This takes time and commitment. In particular it requires teachers to loosen their control. But encouraging children to think for themselves and ask questions was found to have implications for children's behaviour that went beyond project work. And as we note in Maynard et al. (2013b) when supporting Reggio-inspired projects, the increased space and its distance from the classroom meant that children were already more able to resist their teacher's attempts at regulation – it was easier to keep out of their teacher's sight and away from their reach!

More significantly, perhaps, relinquishing control was seen as extremely difficult when teachers felt under pressure to meet targets and outcomes.

Across our projects this commitment was evidenced in, for example, the sup-plementing of project work with the direct teaching of factual knowledge and basic skills (Maynard and Chicken 2010); and in an increasingly tight focus on subject-based outcomes when teaching time was constrained (for example, by preparations for Christmas) (Maynard et al. 2011). We noted also that the some teachers felt uncomfortable about allowing children to follow their interests and develop theories when these were 'inaccurate', or to pursue themes that crossed subject disciplines, and maintained that there had been a great deal of discussion about 'when to tell children the correct information' (Maynard and Chicken 2010: 35).

What is also important to note is that it was the outdoor environment that appeared to be associated with child-centred approaches and that 'child-initiated' activities outdoors did not appear to be as highly valued as subject-based work undertaken in the classroom; we observed in project three, for example, that the teacher remained inside the classroom focusing on the direct or indirect teaching of subject content while support staff were sent outside to supervise children's play (Maynard et al. 2011). We therefore concluded that while teachers expressed their commitment to child-centred approaches, their professional identities, as embedded within the classroom, could better be described as 'subject centred'. In this way, the teachers appeared to be raising ideological as well as professional objections to supporting 'child-initiated' activity outdoors.

Conclusion

In this chapter I have argued that 'child-initiated' activity has many benefits for children: for example, it supports children's sense of self-determination (Deci and Ryan 2002), their creative thinking (Robson and Rowe 2012) and their posi-tive learning dispositions – including a 'mastery orientation' towards learning (Dweck 2000) – through the provision of a 'potentiating' environment (Claxton and Carr 2004); however, supporting such activity requires teachers to develop complex cognitive skills, including the ability to loosen control. It was the par-ticular 'features', 'affordance of space' and 'associations' of the natural outdoor environment that enabled the teachers more easily to do this so also enabling the children to assert their agency within a rich, supportive and challenging context.

In terms of the Foundation Phase, it is important to recognize that 'child-initiated' learning is only one approach advocated – teachers are also required to undertake some direct teaching. But if they are to develop the cognitive skills that are required to support 'child-initiated' activity – to support children in constructing and exploring their own theories of the world – Foundation Phase teachers will need to recognize the child as a competent learner and the particular benefits that 'child-initiated' activity and the natural outdoor envi-ronment have to offer. They need to loosen the ties of a subject-centred identity a little. And if they are able to do so, they may recognize that subject knowledge is not irrelevant; as the teachers in my study nearly twenty years ago discovered (although approaching this from the opposite direction) sensitive and 'informed' questions and provocations – of the kind suggested by Froebel and Plowden – not only can support children's social and emotional development and wellbeing but also can take children on a path that leads to later understandings of many key concepts and processes.

References

ACCAC (2000) *Desirable Outcomes for Children's Learning before Compulsory School Age.* Cardiff: ACCAC.

Alexander, R., Rose, J. and Woodhead, C. (1992) *Currriculum Organisation and Classroom Practice in Primary Schools: A Discussion Paper.* London: Department for Education and Science.

Bilton, H. (2010) *Outdoor Learning in the Early Years: Management and Innovation,* 3rd edn. London: Taylor and Francis.

Bruce, T. (2011) *Early Childhood Education,* 4th edn. London: Hodder Education.

CACE (Central Advisory Council for Education) (1967) *Children and Their Primary Schools* (Plowden Report). London: HMSO.

Claxton, G. and Carr, M. (2004) A framework for teaching learning: the dynamics of disposition, *Early Years,* 24(1): 87–97.

Cox, C.B. and Dyson, A.E. (eds) (1971) *The Black Papers on Education.* London: Davis Poynter Ltd.

Craft, A.T., Cremin, T., Burnard, P. and Chappell, K. (2008) Possibility thinking with children in England aged 3–7. In A.T. Craft, T. Cremin and P. Burnard (eds) *Creative Learning and How We Document It.* Stoke on Trent: Trentham Books.

DCELLS (2008a) *Framework for Children's Learning for 3–7 year olds in Wales.* Cardiff: Welsh Assembly Government.

DCELLS (2008b) *Play/Active Learning: Overview For 3 to 7 Year Olds.* Cardiff: Welsh Assembly Government.

DCELLS (2008c) *Learning and Teaching Pedagogy.* Cardiff: Welsh Assembly Government.

Deci, E.L. and Ryan, R.M. (2002) *Handbook of Self-Determination Research.* Rochester, NY: University of Rochester Press.

Dweck, C.S. (2000) *Self-theories: Their Role in Motivation, Personality and Development.* Hove: Psychology Press.

Fjørtoft, I. (2004) Landscape as playscape: the effects of natural environments on children's play and motor development, *Children, Youth and Environments,* 14(2): 21–44. doi: http://www.colorado.edu/journals/cye/ (accessed 6 January 2014).

Gandini, L. (1993) Fundamentals of the Reggio Emilia approach to early childhood education, *Young Children,* November: 4–8.

Hadow, W.H. (1931) *Report of the Consultative Committee on The Primary School* (The Hadow Report). London: HMSO.

Kaplan, S. (1995) The restorative benefits of nature: toward an integrative framework, *Journal of Environmental Psychology*, 15: 169–82.

Kuo, F.E. and Taylor, A.F. (2004) A potential natural treatment for attention deficit/ hyperactivity disorder: evidence from a national study, *American Journal of Public Health*, September, 94(9): 1580–6.

Kwon, Y. (2002) Changing curriculum for early childhood education in England, *Early Childhood Research and Practice*, 4(2). http://ecrp.uiuc.edu/v4n2/kwon. html (accessed 6 January 2013).

Lester, S. and Maudsley, M. (2007) *Play, Naturally: A Review of Children's Natural Play*. London: Play England.

Lindon, J. (2013) *Child-initiated Learning: Positive Relationships in the Early Years*. London: Mark Allen Group.

Little, H. and Eager, D. (2010) Risk, challenge and safety: implications for play quality and playground design, *European Early Childhood Research Journal*, 18(4): 497–513. doi: 10.1080/1350293X.2010.525949

Malaguzzi, L. (1993) For an education based on relationships, *Young Children*, 49(1): 9–12.

Maynard, T. (1996) The missing element? Early years teachers' attitudes towards subject knowledge, in T.Cox (ed.) *The National Curriculum and the Early Years*. London: Falmer Press.

Maynard, T. (2007) Encounters with Forest School and Foucault: a risky business, *Education 3–13*, 35(4): 379–91.

Maynard, T. and Chicken, S. (2010) Through a different lens: exploring Reggio Emilia in a Welsh context, *Early Years: An International Research Journal*, 30(1): 29–39.

Maynard, T., Taylor, C., Waldron, S. et al. (2013a) *Evaluating the Foundation Phase: Policy Logic Model and Programme Theory*. Cardiff: Welsh Government.

Maynard, T., Waters, J. and Clement, J. (2011) Moving outdoors: further explorations of child-led learning in a Welsh context, *Education 3–13*, 41(3): 282–99. http://www.tandfonline.com/doi/full/10.1080/03004279.2011.578750 (accessed 6 January 2014).

Maynard, T., Waters, J. and Clement, J. (2013b) Child-initiated learning, the outdoor environment and the 'underachieving' child, *Early Years: An International Research Journal*, 33(3): 212–25. doi:10.1080/09575146.2013.771152

McInnes, K., Howard, J., Miles, G.E. and Crowley, K. (2011) Differences in practitioners understanding of play and how this influences pedagogy and children's perceptions of play, *Early Years: An International Research Journal*, 31(2): 121–33.

Moser, T. and Martinsen, M.T. (2010) The outdoor environment in Norwegian kindergartens as pedagogical space for toddlers' play, learning and development, *European Early Childhood Education Research Journal*, 18(4): 457–71.

NAfW (2001) *The Learning Country*. Cardiff: National Assembly for Wales.

NAfW (2003) *The Learning Country: Foundation Phase – 3 to 7 years*. Cardiff: National Assembly for Wales.

Nicholson, S. (1971) How NOT to cheat children: the theory of loose parts, *Landscape Architecture*, 62(1): 30–4.

O'Hear, A. (1991) Transcript of BBC Radio 'File on 4', 19 February 1991.

Ouvry, M. (2003) *Exercising Muscles and Minds*. London: National Children's Bureau.

Pramling Samuelsson, I. and Johansson, E. (2006) Play and learning – inseparable dimensions in preschool practice, *Early Child Development and Care*, 176(1): 47–65.

Rinaldi, C. (1998) Projected curriculum constructed through documentation – progettazione; an interview with Lella Gandini, in C. Edward, L. Gandini and G. Forman (eds) *The Hundred Languages of Children: The Reggio Emilia Approach – Advanced Reflections*. New York: Ablex Publishing Corporation.

Rivkin, M. (1995) *The Great Outdoors: Restoring Children's Right to Play Outside*. Washington, DC: National Association for the Education of Young Children (NAEYC).

Robson, S. and Rowe, V. (2012) Observing young children's creative thinking: engagement, involvement and persistence, *International Journal of Early Years Education*, 20(4): 349–64.

Sandseter, E.B.H. (2007) Categorising risky play: how can we identify risk-taking in children's play? *European Early Childhood Education Research Journal*, 15(2): 237–52.

Sandseter, E.B.H. (2009) Children's expressions of exhilaration and fear in risky play, *Contemporary Issues in Early Childhood*, 10(2): 92–106.

Santer, J., Griffiths, C. and Goodall, D. (2007) *Free Play in Early Childhood: A Literature Review*. London: National Children's Bureau.

SCAA (School Curriculum Assessment Authority) (1996) *Nursery Education: Desirable Outcomes for Children's Learning on Entering Compulsory Education*. London: SCAA and Department for Education and Employment.

Sobel, D. (1993) *Children's Special Places: Exploring the Role of Forts, Dens and Bush Houses in Middle Childhood*. Tucson, AZ: Zephyr Press.

Soler, J. and Miller, L. (2003) The struggle for early childhood curricula: a comparison of the English Foundation Stage Curriculum, *Te Whāriki* and Reggio Emilia, *International Journal of Early Years Education*, 11(1): 57–67.

Stephenson, A. (2002) Opening up the outdoors: exploring the relationship between the indoor and outdoor environment of a centre, *European Early Childhood Education Research Journal*, 10(1): 29–38.

Sternberg, R.J. (2003) Creative thinking in the classroom, *Scandinavian Journal of Educational Research*, 47(3): 325–38.

Tovey, H. (2007) *Playing Outdoors: Spaces and Places, Risk and Challenge*. Maidenhead: McGraw Hill.

Trawick-Smith, J. (1994) *Interactions in the Classroom: Facilitating Play in the Early Years*. New York: MacMillan Publishing Co.

Tuan, Yi-Fu (1977) *Space and Place: The Perspective of Experience.* Minneapolis, MN: The University of Minnesota Press.

Waite, S., Davies, B. and Brown, K. (2006) *Five Stories of Outdoor Learning from Settings for 2–11 Year Olds in Devon.* Plymouth: University of Plymouth.

Waters, J. and Begley, A. (2007) Supporting the development of risk-taking behaviours in the early years: an exploratory study, *Education 3–13*, 35(4): 365–77.

Waters J. and Maynard, T. (2010) What's so interesting outside? A study of child-initiated interaction in the natural outdoor environment, *European Early Childhood Education Research Journal*, 18(4): 473–83.

Wells, N.M. and Evans, G.W. (2003) Nearby nature: a buffer of life stress among rural children, *Environment and Behaviour*, 35(3): 311–30.

Wood, E. (2010a) Reconceptualising the play-pedagogy relationship: from control to complexity, in L. Brooker and S. Edwards (eds) *Engaging Play.* Maidenhead: Open University Press.

Wood, E. (2010b) Developing integrated pedagogical approaches to play and learning, in P. Broadhead, J. Howard and E. Wood (eds) *Play and Learning in the Early Years: From Research to Practice.* London: Sage.

5 Risky outdoor play: embracing uncertainty in pursuit of learning

Sue Waite, Valerie Huggins and Karen Wickett

In this chapter, we critically consider why early years practitioners should aim to give children ample opportunity to play outdoors during their early years and some of the 'risks' associated with this. We argue that criticality is important since some literature on outdoor play and learning is evangelical and may not consider potentially adverse facets (Pratt 2011). We begin by defining the concepts associated with risk, hazard, danger and challenge, to clarify that risk per se is not necessarily negative. We then link this to temporally and culturally situated conceptualizations of childhood to examine how underlying views of 'the child' shape the provision that adults are willing to provide for them. Why outdoor spaces may present particular issues regarding risk is discussed, considering both adult and child perspectives on learning outside. We argue that risk is an inherent part of the learning process and that outdoor contexts can support learning in a number of uniquely different ways, leading us to reflect critically on issues related to preparation for and management of risky outdoor play. We conclude our argument with the suggestion that UK practitioners face a delicate balancing act between competing values associated with child protection, child-centred learning and challenge.

Is risk a bad thing?

In western societies that are, arguably, dominated by a 'culture of fear' (Furedi 2002), the term 'risk' is often used interchangeably with 'danger' or 'hazard' and generally has a negative connotation; however, according to some commentators, 'risk' can express situations where there is simply an uncertainty about outcome, whether positive or negative (Little and Eager 2010). Thus we might argue that allowing children to play outdoors represents a *good* risk if we consider that beneficial outcomes (eftec 2011) outweigh the potential for harm. The Health and Safety Executive (HSE) define risk as the chance that 'somebody could be harmed by a hazard together with an indication of how serious the harm could be' (HSE 2011: 2). Hazards are defined as 'potential sources of harm' (Ball et al. 2008: 29) but since hazards exist in all aspects of life, encountering them and learning to deal with them are important for children. Danger, however, describes hazardous situations that are likely to cause unacceptable harm unless removed or managed. The discourse about risk centres principally on physical harm (Ball et al. 2008) but it is important to recognize that children (like adults) not only take physical risks but also encounter risks on a daily basis in our thinking, in social situations and in our emotional responses (Papasterphanou 2006). So, riskiness is part of everyday life and has potentially good but uncertain outcomes. As these uncertainties pervade life itself, it is important that children learn how to prepare for and manage risks themselves in order to live full lives that are resilient in the face of setbacks and mistakes (Gill 2009). Louv (2010) argues that children's disconnection from unpredictable nature is leading them to be cut off not only from the natural world but also from their responsibility for themselves (p. 129). In the next section we consider how this situation may have arisen.

Concepts of the child and childhood

Children within contemporary western society are depicted as in need of protection but also feared as out of control (Matthews and Limb 1999). Concerns over young people's antisocial behaviour and children's safety in public space have been associated with the decreasing amount of time spent by children in the outdoors (Sutton 2008). An ambivalent attitude to childhood is not new. Ariès (1962) suggests that it was not until the eighteenth century that the notion of childhood as a distinct period of life was constructed and before this time, children were not perceived as different to adults, merely smaller people. Alternative complex concepts of children coexist, positioning them variously as innocents who naturally become good people if left to their own devices, as vulnerable and impotent, and as potential delinquents who needed to be trained into proper behaviour (Wood and Attfield 1996). In this section we discuss how the construct of the child continues to influence adult attitudes towards risk-taking in play.

A preoccupation with attempting to eliminate the possibility of harm to all children is a relatively modern phenomenon. By the late nineteenth century, social reform impulses had led the middle and upper classes in the UK to become concerned about working-class children found in dangerous and unhealthy working conditions (Hendrick 1997). This anxiety resulted in an outcry to save these children from inappropriate adult influences and environments; schooling to train young minds was seen as a significant strategy to protect them. The Education Acts of the 1870s and 1880s enabled all children over 5 to attend school. The concept of children at risk and in need of protection continues to be central to Western perspectives (Philo 2011) despite contemporaneous attention to children's rights and capabilities to have a say in their lives (Clark, MacQuail and Moss 2003). Yet it is also increasingly acknowledged that macro-level constraints such as poverty, political, societal and familial circumstances place significant limitations on children's agency (Mayall 2012). For example, since the 1970s there has been a growing anxiety among parents in the UK about perceived dangers in the environment, such as traffic and dangerous strangers (Selwyn 2000), despite a lack of evidence of any greater incidence of accidents (Ball et al. 2008). This has resulted in greater organization and supervision of children's activities (Selwyn 2000), which tend to limit children's opportunities to control their own play and to experience freedom. The 'new' sociology of childhood that arose in the mid-1980s argued for viewing children as competent actors and stimulated movements to establish child-centred research methods and greater participation for children in making decisions that affect them (Clark and Moss 2001). Benwell (2013), however, cautions that a more nuanced understanding of what freedom and risk represent in different cultures is needed and that the current preponderance of child-centred approaches and emphasis on the children's agency misses important relational and societal aspects of children's security in some communities. Furthermore, Tisdall and Punch (2012) question the new sociology of childhood's response to former Piagetian developmental views of childhood in placing undue emphasis on children's agency, competence and participation. This, they argue, has led to uncritical accounts of a universal child's voice that ignores the situated societal influences that shape discourses open to children and adults in different contexts, particularly in Majority World settings. International policy and values enshrined in the United Nations Convention on the Rights of the Child (UNCRC) support the rights of children everywhere to play (see Article 31) and for their schooling to develop respect for the natural environment (Article 29), but this vision of a globalized child may obscure more subtle pressures and influences in particular contexts (Tisdall and Punch 2012: 257).

It is with this complexity in mind that we turn now to current constructs of the child in the UK. The English Early Years Foundation Stage (EYFS) represents children as 'competent and capable' (Principles into Practice card, DFE 2012), which is in line with the 'new' sociology of childhood view. Across the border in Wales, the Foundation Phase for children 3–7 years is also underpinned by the belief that children are competent and active learners as it states children have a 'natural curiosity to explore and learn through first-hand experiences' (WAG 2008 p: 6). In Scotland, the Pre-birth to Three: Positive Outcomes for Scotland's Children and Families recognizes that practitioners should believe 'children to be competent individuals' (Learning and Teaching Scotland 2010: 32) who are capable learners. Yet, in the Scottish Early Years Framework, for children from birth to 8 years old, competent and capable children are not mentioned. Instead the Framework is driven by the belief every child and their family have a 'right' to effective early years provision and early intervention (Scottish Government 2008), so empowering children to reach their full potential; however, the historical culture of 'doing things for or to people' (Scottish Government 2011: 2), can in fact limit children's agency (Deacon 2011).

Hence, it could be argued that the value of outdoor play for children's health, wellbeing and education (Garrick 2009), which features in the English EYFS theme, 'Enabling Environments', throughout The Foundation Phase in Wales and as mentioned above in the Scottish Frameworks, may be undermined by competing constructs pertaining to child protection and children's vulnerability. This theme not only recognizes that the outside is central to some children's learning but also emphasizes that practitioners should provide challenging experiences for children. As the child is perceived as competent, to some extent they are regarded as being able to manage their own risks. Nonetheless, we now go on to critically examine whether this official discourse accurately represents the enactment of practice for children and current constructs of children in society. We highlight how other influences impinge on how policy and guidance is played out in attitudes and practice related to risky play.

Since the late 1980s there has also been a growing emphasis upon health and safety regulations and a perceived growth in the number of complaints and even litigation in the event of any harm occurring to a child (Gill 2009), although actual levels of accidents through adventurous play are low compared to other activities (Ball et al. 2008: 11). Yet Gill (2009) suggests that certain types of risk help children to learn through mastering practical activities and managing risk to keep themselves safe. Furthermore, he argues that children have a 'natural appetite' for risk and challenge which is 'an essential part of living a meaningful and satisfying life' (Gill 2009: 16). In the next section, we consider what risky outdoor play offers in meeting that 'natural appetite'.

Reasons to support risky outdoor play

Outdoor spaces and the natural environment are full of loose parts and unpredictable elements (Stephenson 2003). This makes them inherently risky (Sandseter 2009), but also means that they are rich in affordances for thinking, moving and interacting (Fjørtoft 2001). They offer a canvas and range of materials that can be used more flexibly and freely than indoors because they are less constrained by rules and expectations about how you use them (Waite, Evans and Rogers 2011; see also Waters, Chapter 7, this volume). Many more types of materials and equipment can be accommodated outside than inside. There is also scope to do things on a big scale and to use bulky materials such as crates, planks, large bricks, etc. which are usually impracticable within a building. Although these may be considered hazardous by some practitioners, Bundy et al. (2009) found that no more accidents occurred when large scale loose parts were introduced to the playground than beforehand but that teachers noted greater social interaction and creativity in play. Thus children gain opportunities to develop their independence (Waite et al. 2013), their decision-making (Mental Health Foundation 1999; Waite 2013) and their self-protection strategies (Sandseter and Kennair 2011). Children's attitudes and values are powerfully influenced by their early social and cultural experiences and it is extremely difficult to recover the enthusiasm for exploration and discovery which is a natural feature of children in the earliest years (Kellert and Kahn 2002) if this has been stifled and discouraged by overregulation and overprotection at this age (Carson 1998; Sobel 2004; Louv 2010). Exploration can effectively be supported outdoors by natural environments (Fjørtoft 2001), different pedagogies (Waite 2011) and open-ended resources (Tovey 2007).

Moreover, children need challenges if they are to develop their abilities to their full potential (Smith 2010). Outdoor play is a crucial area of challenge for children of this age because in outdoor spaces they are more likely to set their own levels of challenge and engage in imaginative play than inside classrooms (Rogers and Evans 2008). Observation has also shown that children are extremely adept at self-direction in outdoor places (White 2008; Kelly and White 2013). Children themselves attribute riskiness in play to attempting something never done before; feeling almost 'out of control', and overcoming fear (Stephenson 2003: 36), thus their subjective emotions appear more central to their experience of risk and challenge than actual physical features. They are also very good, in familiar circumstances, at being aware of what they can and cannot manage (p. 36), although experienced practitioners are familiar with the need to remove some opportunities and materials from children who are less likely to be able to differentiate between a hazard or challenge. Children are often operating at the edge of their capabilities when engaging in play as they trial different ways of being and behaving (Waite and Rees 2013), and may experience accidents and setbacks (Waite et al. 2013); however, small discomforts and occasional lack of success are key learning tools in the development of their resilience (Ball et al. 2008).

Anyone who has stood at a setting door at break time will be aware of the excitement engendered as children leave the building for outdoor play (Waite and Rea 2007). Since it is a human characteristic to find challenging and slightly risky activities pleasurable, many children deliberately seek out thrills and scares (Gill 2009). Well-managed outdoor environments include some risky elements such as heights to climb that children are able to self-assess relative to their own competence and confidence. At the same time, hazards that are dangerous and less obvious to children such as faulty equipment should be minimized or excluded (Ball et al. 2008; White 2008). The previous UK government's policy was clear that taking risks is part of children's learning to be safe (DCSF 2008).

Meeting of challenges through exploration leads to a strong sense of personal achievement (Knight 2009). Arguably this is most powerful when the goal and challenge is also self set (Corsaro 2003). If what children do in a setting is always highly restricted, controlled and monitored by adults, then their sense of achievement may be limited and narrowly defined; doing what is expected of them may close down children's creative learning opportunities (Waite and Davis 2007). Managing reasonable risks and dealing with setbacks can result in positive dispositions towards learning (Athey 2009; Dweck 2000; Huggins and

Wickett 2011) and high self-motivation (Katz 1995). Paradoxically, a 'no-risk' approach may endanger the child's sense of him- or herself as a learner and as a capable person.

Conversely, Forest School pedagogy is based upon breaking skills down into small steps so that children do not experience failure (Waite, Davis and Brown 2006). This raises a question about the nature of risk in Forest School and the role of the adult in managing that. It may be that Forest School environment is very unfamiliar to many children today, or that Forest School is often directed towards children who have experienced difficulties within mainstream provision and have low resilience in the face of failure, so this is seen as a way to build self-confidence (Knight 2009). In either case, it points once more to the need for nuanced and situated conceptualizations of children (Benwell 2013) to inform a variety of provision for and management of risk within play. Apart from wider sociocultural differences, inclusive practitioners organize play provision so that all children can potentially have access. Yet individual children have very different experience of exploring situations independently, of taking decisions and managing risk, as well as different propensities for taking risks (Little and Wyver 2010). Some will already be skilled and used to tackling new situations and challenges. Others, perhaps inexperienced, inhibited or hitherto overprotected, may need greater protection from the consequences of ill-judged actions and support to develop their confidence to try new things. Such individual differences must always be borne in mind.

> The capacity for teachers to support toddlers and young children effectively is not so much in the challenges that the environment or even the children offer, but in the intentionality of the teachers to promote learning. We concluded that a deep knowledge of the particular environment including the weather, opportunities alongside potential risks and the nature and culture of the place supports intentional teaching. A second key consideration is developmental knowledge of individual children.
>
> (Kelly and White 2013: 9)

Playing outdoors offers exposure to a range of natural conditions, particularly weather and its consequences. For a significant number of small children today their exposure to weather may have been very limited because of travelling by car, or being pushed in buggies with all-enveloping plastic covers, and swathed in modern fabrics for clothing (Huggins and Wickett 2011). For some children, a setting offering the opportunity of being outside in almost all weather conditions can provide a missing sensory experience. Furthermore, variations in weather conditions also produce substantial elements of change and unpredictability in a familiar environment. They may contain new challenges and make new demands. For example, the soil after rain is heavy and sticky, and children digging in it clearly experience a different challenge to digging in clean sand in the tray indoors. Moreover, they may encounter stones, roots and minibeasts, which both test their abilities and enlarge their awareness. Many outdoor contexts provide rich experiential opportunities for learning about and managing the physical environment, including negotiating irregularities, slopes and hills and investigating holes, the textures of soil and stone and growing things. In planning for and preparing an outside area, practitioners can consider the range of opportunities possible within the resources, terrain and the design, to maximize possibilities for exploration. Exploring the unknown and the unpredictable provides the possibility of multi-sensory surprises, which frequently lead to memorable learning (Waite 2007). Outside, children can learn to recognize patterns within such variety, make sense of them, predict and be able to organize and adjust their own behaviour accordingly (Tovey 2007).

Being outside affords a greater sense of space, together with a freedom from some of the constraints of behaviour inside (Rogers and Evans 2008). Obvious and conventional opportunities to run, jump, chase and shout are offered by the outside space but so are less tangible freedoms and satisfactions, such as the opportunity to hide away from adult gaze and to negotiate with peers without interference from adults (Waite, Rogers and Evans 2013). Thus, physical risk is only one dimension of what needs to be considered in assessing an outdoor environment's opportunities and challenges for particular groups of children.

It is also important that we create a culture of appropriate risk-taking that is ethical and socially responsible. Much of the discussion around risk is centred on individual harm and current neoliberal maxims underpinning education can result in individualism (Bialostok and Kamberelis 2010). Individual resilience is a necessary disposition to foster in the early years so that children are able to adapt during their life course in an ever changing uncertain world (Bialostok and Kamberelis 2010); however, rather than outdoor play only 'produc[ing] children as risk-takers, who aspire toward autonomy, who are "enterprising selves" and who strive toward personal fulfilment through acts of choice' (p. 300), we argue that they should also be learning about the potential consequences for themselves and others as they take risks through peer interactions and contingent support of adults (Waite, Rogers and Evans 2013).

Overall, the reasons outlined above suggest that we should accept an element of risk in play for children's benefit. But how do we decide what level of risk is acceptable? We return to the notion of balance between risk, the likelihood of suffering harm and beneficial possible outcomes. We certainly do not suggest allowing children to undertake activities with a significant likelihood of harm (Huggins and Wickett 2011) but simply that their play should not be circumscribed or prevented by adult concerns to remove the slightest possibility of something going wrong. A deficit view of the child as incapable of taking care of themselves is implied if an adult hovers anxiously and utters a string of warnings and instructions, and this is highly likely either to inhibit the play or to lead children to abdicate responsibility for the anticipated accident.

To summarize, 'In essence, play is a safe and beneficial activity. Sensible adult judgements are all that is generally required to derive the best benefits to children whilst ensuring that they are not exposed to unnecessary risk' (HSE 2012: 2). In the following section we consider what steps might be taken to make these sensible judgements.

Some challenges and risks for practitioners

No amount of individual awareness and care of environmental conditions can entirely eliminate an element of risk in children's play. Practitioners are accustomed to making thorough risk assessments in order to identify potential hazards and to reduce the likelihood that these will cause serious harm (see the section below for further guidance on this). Yet, it is impossible for adults, however rigorous, to eliminate all possibility of injury if they are going to allow children some independence and an element of control in their play. This can be unnerving for some practitioners. Not only does it increase the level of unpredictability in situations, and acknowledge limitations on the degree of control they can exercise over outdoor play, but it may also require a shift in their understanding of the adult's role when teaching young children. As we have discussed earlier, current conceptualizations of the child are complex and mixed (Tisdall and Punch 2012). Despite EYFS guidance being largely based upon the new sociology of childhood, some enacted practice may still draw on developmental views of children as vulnerable (King 2007) coupled with fears about blame in the case of accidents (Ball et al. 2008). In respecting the children's agenda and acknowledging that risks should be balanced against potential benefits, adults need to cede some assessment of risk to the children themselves, thus better preparing them for understanding of their limitations *and* importantly for developing their confidence, competence and capabilities (Moss and Petrie 2002).

Bundy et al. warn that, 'In seeking to protect children from all possible harm, surplus safety is working to eliminate the benefits associated with exciting, challenging and stimulating play' (2009: 35). Practitioners' negative actions and attitudes can have a detrimental consequence on a child, not only encouraging fearfulness but even inviting negative outcomes because children cede responsibility for taking sufficient care of themselves (p. 35). Leadership needs to establish a whole setting approach where responsibility for learning and safety is shared and appropriate balances between challenge and risk are carefully considered and agreed. For instance, Waters and Begley (2007) found that children sometimes receive different messages from staff about what is safe and what is not, leading to a lack of clarity about responsibilities. A negotiated but common standard, taking children's capabilities and attitudes into account, such as that promoted within Forest School practice, can result in greater clarity about risk and how to manage it. This is of particular importance because practitioners may well have subtly different perceptions and attitudes towards risk, which can significantly affect how they approach outdoor play. A common approach will support understanding of responsible risk-taking by children and staff. Leaders should ensure that, wherever practicable, the responsibility for managing risk is also shared with the children as this will allow them to develop better judgement about the likelihood of harm from risky activities. For example, when children use heavy, large bricks, adults and children can discuss safe ways of carrying and using them, such as asking a friend to help carry a large brick or using both hands to transport it.

This negotiation highlights that, as with other aspects of early years provision, leadership needs to establish team approaches based upon appropriate theory and research, rather than taken-for-granted ideas. For example, despite evidence that boys in fact suffer more injuries in risky play situations, both boys and girls consider girls more exposed to danger from risky play and practitioners tend to be more protective of girls and more restrictive of their physical play (Little and Wyver 2010). In the following section, a possible framework for supporting a whole-setting approach to responsible risk-taking is outlined.

Preparing for and managing risky play

Preparation for risky play situations should always start from a clear outdoor play policy which includes the identification and assessment of benefits as well as associated risks. The hazards that may arise in connection with the setting or activity require careful analysis, which involves considering any possible harm to:

- the child
- others
- the provider.

This latter category refers to the possibility of litigation if the practitioner's or organization's duty of care is not observed; however, the first consideration should be what benefits risky play may have for the children. So in preparing for risky play, settings and practitioners should take the following steps:

1   develop a policy framework for outdoor play that draws out the various benefits that it can have for children and how the site and staff will support those;
2   construct a written risk/benefit analysis of the environment and activities;
3   carry out regular inspections of the environment and reviews of activities;
4   ensure staff are involved in the development of policy and risk assessment and are therefore well placed to engage with in-the-moment interventions during activities (dynamic risk assessment);

5   include children and parents in ongoing dialogue about appropriate balance between benefits and risks.

Preparing a risk/benefit assessment

There are three key factors to consider and balance when deciding whether a risk is acceptable:

1   Likelihood of children coming to harm
2   Severity of that harm
3   Benefits, rewards or outcomes of that activity for the children

(Ball et al. 2008: 114)

Table 5.1 sets out a framework for the points to consider.

Table 5.1   Framework for a risk/benefit assessment to support risky play

Issue	Comments	Evidence/sources
Benefits	Outline the reasons why an activity is planned and how children will benefit from it	Research Experience Children's interests
Risks	Identify the risks of harm and evaluate how serious and likely they are	Experience Other similar situations
Expert opinion	Advice from experts if appropriate	Specialist reports
Local factors	Other environmental and social factors that might affect decision	Local knowledge of place, individual children, values regarding children's learning
Options	List possible ways to proceed to manage risks	Experience
Risk/benefit judgement	Weigh up benefits and risks to choose optimal compromise	Discussion with staff, possibly parents, knowledgeable others, children
Implementation	Action taken	Whole-setting awareness
Review	Date for next review	Use knowledge from this risk/ benefit analysis and any incidents to inform next review

Source: adapted from Ball et al. 2008:71

Managing risky play

Risk/benefit analysis therefore involves balancing the duty to protect children from avoidable serious harm and the duty to provide stimulating and challenging learning environments. Carrying out appropriate written risk/benefit assessments on a regular basis and involving all staff and children in the review will help to make the environment a safer place for all by spreading responsibility sensibly and appropriately among those involved. The process is ongoing and dynamic and involves creating a suitable balance between protection of the child and suitable levels of challenge for learning that build upon children's interests and capabilities. Balanced decision-making involves assessing whether the level of risk is tolerable, what measures could be taken to mitigate the risk, the relative potential costs compared to benefits and the risks of unforeseen related consequences of taking or not taking certain actions. These considerations are vital to ensure that risky play supports good learning opportunities in a responsible way. Further useful guidance on risk management can be found in Beames et al. (2012: 77–92).

In the final section below, we summarize our argument that risky play should be welcomed in order to benefit all children and that inherent uncertainties offer children important learning opportunities that careful whole-setting approaches can successfully prepare for and manage.

Embracing uncertainty in pursuit of learning

In this chapter we have problematized discourse around risk in relation to differing but contemporaneous conceptualizations of childhood, arguing that adopting a fixed view of the universal child fails to acknowledge the messiness and complexity of situated, cultural and individual responses to risk and security. Although UK practitioners are guided in documentation by sociocultural and constructionist views of young children's learning, in practice, fear of criticism for lack of care coupled with continuing developmental underrating of children's capabilities may combine so that provision for risky play lacks a strong theoretical rationale. One way to overcome this might be for practitioners and settings to make processes of preparing for and managing risky play more visible and open to debate so that educational and societal values for risky play and their relationship to different conceptualizations of childhood held by staff, parents and the wider community are made explicit. A possible framework for this process is suggested. Including children in negotiation allows further tailoring of what are acceptable risks and appropriate challenges for individuals in specific contexts. In this way, the uncertainties that are inherent in risky play can be embraced in pursuit of quality learning opportunities for all children.

References

Ariès, P. (1962) *Centuries of Childhood*. London: Jonathan Cape.

Athey, C. (2009) *Extending Thought in Young Children: A Parent–Teacher Partnership*, 2nd edn. London: Sage.

Ball, D., Gill, T. and Spiegal, B. (2008). *Managing Risk in Play Provision: Implementation Guide*. Nottingham: Department for Children, Schools and Families and Play England.

Beames, S., Higgins, P. and Nicol, R. (2012) *Learning Outside the Classroom: Theory and Guidelines for Practice*. Abingdon: Routledge.

Benwell, M. (2013) Rethinking conceptualisations of adult-imposed restriction and children's experiences of autonomy in outdoor space, *Children's Geographies*, 11(1): 28–43.

Bialostok, S. and Kamberelis, G. (2010) New capitalism, risk and subjectification in an early childhood classroom, *Contemporary Issues in Early Childhood*, 11(3): 299–312.

Bundy, A.C., Luckett, T., Tranter, P.J. et al. (2009) The risk is that there is 'no risk': a simple, innovative intervention to increase children's activity levels, *International Journal of Early Years Education*, 17(1): 33–45.

Carson, R. (1998) *The Sense of Wonder*. New York: Harper Collins.

Clark, A. (2007) A hundred ways of listening: gathering children's perspectives of their early childhood environment, *Young Children*, 62(3): 76–81.

Clark, A., MacQuail, S. and Moss, P. (2003) *Exploring the Field of Listening to and Consulting with Young Children*. Research Report 445. London: DfES.

Clark, A. and Moss, P. (2001) *Listening to Young Children: The Mosaic Approach*. London: National Children's Bureau.

Corsaro, W.A. (2003) *We are Friends, Right?: Inside Kid's Culture*. Washington, DC: Joseph Henry Press.

Deacon, S. (2011) *Joining the Dots: A Better Start for Scotland's Children*. http://www.scotland.gov.uk/Resource/Doc/343337/0114216.pdf (accessed 15 July 2013).

DCSF (2008) *The Early Years Foundation Stage: Principles into Practice Cards*. London: DCSF.

DfE (2012) *Statutory Framework for the Early Years Foundation Stage: Setting the Standards for Learning, Development and Care for Children from Birth to Five*. DfE Cheshire: DfE.

Dweck. C. (2000) *Self-theories: Their Role in Motivation, Personality and Development*. Hove: Psychology Press.

Dweck, C.S. (2006) *Mindset: The New Psychology of Success*. New York: Random House.

eftec (2011) *Assessing the Benefits of Learning Outside the Classroom in Natural Environments*. London: Final Report for King's College London.

Fjørtoft, I. (2001) The natural environment as a playground for children: the impact of outdoor play activities in pre-primary school children, *Early Childhood Education Journal*, 29(2): 111–17.

Furedi, F. (2002) *Culture of Fear: Risk Taking and the Morality of Low Expectations.* London: Continuum.

Garrick, R. (2009) *Playing Outdoors in the Early Years.* London: Continuum.

Gill, T. (2009) *No Fear: Growing Up in a Risk-adverse Society.* London: Calouste Gulbenkian Foundation.

Hendrick, H. (1997) Constructions and reconstructions of British childhood: an interpretative survey, 1800 to the present, in A. James and A. Prout (eds) *Constructing and Reconstructing Childhood,* 2nd edn. London: Routledge Falmer.

HSE (Health and Safety Executive) (2011) *Five Steps to Risk Assessment.* http://www.hse.gov.uk/pubns/indg163.pdf (accessed 26 June 2013).

HSE (2012) *Children's Play and Leisure: Promoting a Balanced Approach.* http://www.hse.gov.uk/entertainment/childrens-play-july-2012.pdf (accessed 20 February 2013).

Huggins, V. and Wickett, K. (2011) Crawling and toddling in the outdoors: very young children's learning, in S. Waite. (ed.) *Children Learning Outside the Classroom: From Birth to Eleven.* London: Sage.

Katz, L. (1995) *Talks with Teachers of Young Children.* Norwood: Ablex.

Kellert, S. and Kahn, P. (eds) (2002) *Children and Nature.* Cambridge, MA: MIT.

Kelly, J. and White, E.J. (2013) *The Ngahere Project: Teaching and Learning Possibilities in Nature Settings.* http://www.waikato.ac.nz/wmier/publications/reports/the-ngahere-project/ (accessed 26 June 2013).

King, M. (2007) The sociology of childhood as scientific communication: observations from a social systems perspective, *Childhood,* 14(2): 193–213.

Knight, S. (2009) *Forest Schools and Outdoor Play in the Early Years.* London: Sage.

Learning and Teaching Scotland (2010) *Pre-birth to Three: Positive Outcomes for Scotland's Children and Families: National Guidance.* http://www.educationscotland.gov.uk/Images/PreBirthTOThreeBooklet_tcm4-633448. pdf (accessed 7 January 2013).

Little, H. and Eager, D. (2010) Risk, challenge and safety: implications for play quality and playground design, *European Early Childhood Education Research Journal,* 18(4): 497–513 .

Little, H. and Wyver, S. (2010) Individual differences in children's risk perception and appraisals in outdoor play environments, *International Journal of Early Years Education,* 18(4): 297–313.

Louv, R. (2010) *Last Child in the Woods: Saving Our Children from Nature Deficit Disorder.* London: Atlantic Books.

Matthews, H. and Limb, M. (1999) Defining an agenda for the geography of children: review and prospect, *Progress in Human Geography,* 23: 61–90.

Mayall, B. (2012) An afterword: some reflections on a seminar series, *Children's Geographies,* 10(3): 347–55.

Mental Health Foundation (1999) *Bright Futures: Promoting Children and Young People's Mental Health.* London: MHF.

Moss, P. and Petrie, P. (2002) *From Children's Services to Children's Spaces: Public Policy, Children and Childhood*. London: Routledge Falmer.

Papasterphanou, M. (2006) Education, risk and ethics, *Ethics and Education*, 1(1): 47–63.

Philo, C. (2011) Foucault, sexuality and when not to listen to children, *Children's Geographies*, 9(2): 123–7.

Pratt, N. (2011) Mathematics outside the classroom, in S. Waite (ed.) *Children Learning Outside the Classroom: From Birth to Eleven*. London: Sage.

Rogers, S. and Evans, J. (2008) *Inside Role Play in Early Childhood Education: Researching Children's Perspectives*. London: Routledge.

Sandseter, E.B.H. (2009) Characteristics of risky play, *Journal of Adventure Education and Outdoor Learning*, 9(1): 3–21.

Sandseter, E.B.H. and Kennair, L.E.O (2011) Children's risky play from an evolutionary perspective: the anti-phobic effects of thrilling experiences, *Evolutionary Psychology*, 9(2): 257–84.

Scottish Government (2008) *The Early Years Framework*. http://www.scotland.gov.uk/Resource/Doc/257007/0076309.pdf (accessed 18 July 2013).

Scottish Government (2011) *The Early Years Framework Progress So Far*. http://www.scotland.gov.uk/Resource/Doc/337715/0110884.pdf (accessed 18 July 2013).

Selwyn, J. (2000) Technologies and environments: new freedoms, new constraints, in M. Boushel, M. Fawcett and J. Selwyn (eds) *Focus on Childhood Principles and Realities*. Oxford: Blackwell Science.

Smith, P.K. (2010) *Children and Play*. Chichester: Wiley-Blackwell.

Sobel, D. (2004) *Place-based Education: Connecting Classrooms and Communities*. Great Barrington, MA: Orion Society.

Stephenson, A. (2003) Physical risk taking: dangerous or endangered? *Early Years*, 23(10): 35–43.

Sutton, L. (2008) The state of play: disadvantage, play and children's well-being, *Social Policy and Society*, 7(4): 537–49.

Tisdall, E.K.M. and Punch, S. (2012) Not so 'new'? Looking critically at childhood studies, *Children's Geographies*, 10(3): 249–64.

Tovey, H. (2007) *Playing Outdoors: Spaces and Places, Risk and Challenges*. Maidenhead: Open University Press.

WAG (Welsh Assembly Government) (2008) *Framework for Children's Learning for 3–7 Year Olds*. Cardiff: WAG.

Waite, S. (2007) 'Memories are made of this': some reflections on outdoor learning and recall, *Education 3–13*, 35(4): 333–47.

Waite, S. (ed.) (2011) *Children Learning Outside the Classroom: From Birth to Eleven*. London: Sage.

Waite, S. (2013) 'Knowing your place in the world': how place and culture support and obstruct educational aims, *Cambridge Journal of Education*, 43(4): 413–33.

Waite, S. and Davis, B. (2007) The contribution of free play and structured activities in Forest School to learning beyond cognition: an English case, in B. Ravn and

N. Kryger (eds) (2007) *Learning Beyond Cognition*. Copenhagen: The Danish University of Education.

Waite, S., Davis, B. and Brown, K. (2006) Final report: *Forest School Principles: Why We Do What We Do*, July, report for funding body EYDCP (zero14plus) and participants. Plymouth: Plymouth University.

Waite, S., Evans, J. and Rogers, S. (2011) A time of change: outdoor learning and pedagogies of transition between Foundation Stage and Year 1, in S. Waite (ed.) *Children Learning Outside the Classroom: From Birth to Eleven*. London: Sage.

Waite, S. and Rea, T. (2007) Enjoying teaching and learning outside the classroom, in D. Hayes (ed.) *Joyful Teaching and Learning in the Primary School*. Exeter: Learning Matters.

Waite, S. and Rees, S. (2013) Practising empathy: enacting alternative perspectives through imaginative play, *Cambridge Journal of Education*, 13(3): 255–76.

Waite, S., Rogers, S. and Evans, J. (2013) Freedom, flow and fairness: exploring how children develop socially at school through outdoor play, *Journal of Adventure Education and Outdoor Learning*, 13(3): 255–76.

Waters, J. and Begley, S. (2007) Supporting the development of risk-taking behaviours in the early years: an exploratory study, *Education 3–13*, 35(4): 365–77.

White, J. (2008) *Playing and Learning Outdoors: Making Provision for High Quality Experiences in the Outdoor Environment*. London: Routledge.

Wood, E. and Attfield, J. (1996) *Play, Learning and the Early Childhood Curriculum*. London: Paul Chapman.

6   Working with Forest Schools

Sara Knight

Introduction

Forest School is becoming a popular way of introducing young children to the wilder world around them, and many nurseries and schools in the UK now aspire to provide Forest School sessions. It is now widely recognized as a valuable developmental tool for children in the Foundation Stage and Key Stage 1 of the English National Curriculum, and is even more strongly linked to curricula in Scotland and Wales. It is still comparatively new and not widely understood; this chapter therefore explores the ethos, principles and practice of Forest School in the UK and places it in its cultural and historical context. It considers the importance of wilder spaces to children's sense of place, to their engagement with their environment, and to their confidence as agents in control of their own space. This is linked to current thinking being shared by the Forest School Association (2013) in the UK, and the key principles that this thinking reveals. An aspect that causes concerns for many practitioners is around the management of risk, so inevitably there is some discussion of the benefits of risk-taking in healthy child development.

The origins of Forest School in the UK

It was a trip to Denmark in 1994 by the early years department at Bridgwater College that started the development of Forest School in the UK. What they saw in Denmark were groups of children playing outside in woodland: 'The children set their own agenda, cook [on open fires – author's note], listen to storytelling, sing songs and explore at their own level. They are able to climb very high into the trees on rope ladders and swings, and sit and whittle sticks with knives, alone' (Trout 2004: 16).

Bridgwater College staff and students returned inspired, and began to develop what we now know as Forest School, running Forest School sessions for their own college nursery children. Having developed a system for their early years children, they then offered Forest School sessions to students with special needs at the college, and eventually it became part of the provision for other students in the college. There were benefits to the students' self-esteem, confidence and wellbeing: outcomes that were later addressed in the 'Every Child Matters' agenda (Department for Education and Schools 2003).

The Forest School idea quickly became popular with early years practitioners. Bridgwater College's level three course became the standard qualification for practitioners wishing to run Forest School sessions. There was an early replication of the Forest School idea at the Burnworthy Outdoor Education Centre, also in Somerset. The work at this centre expanded to include school refusers, excluded children, women's refuge groups and others. The centre revised and updated the original course, through the Open College Network (OCN), and this in turn was passed on to most of the major training providers in the UK. A part of the Forest School ethos is that it should be delivered by trained practitioners, in order to ensure consistency of delivery and an understanding of the key elements, explained below.

The Forestry Commission recognized the potential importance of Forest School, and they supported the spread of Forest Schools across the UK. This was most evident in Wales where, together with support from the (then) Welsh Assembly, they funded several successful projects, including the work carried out jointly by the New Economics Foundation and the Forestry Commission (Murray 2003). This study was then replicated with reports published in 2005, 2006 and 2007 (Murray and O'Brien 2005; O'Brien and Murray 2006, 2007). These documents put forward a strong case for making Forest School more widely available, and the study has also been replicated in Scotland (Borradaile 2006) with similar results, and by myself (Knight 2013).

I have become convinced that Forest School offers a unique opportunity for children to experience the outdoors in a way that facilitates their holistic development and fosters their growth as confident and competent learners, and also encourages healthy habits and lifestyles (Knight 2013). I have growing concerns that many children were and are being hustled through the most important phase of their education, namely the years from birth to 7, and with an inappropriate emphasis on formal education and conformity to classroom behaviours (Brierley 1994). I am not alone in this; other thinkers and writers in early years education internationally are questioning our approach to educating the under 7s (Yelland 2005).

Scandinavian connections

There may be an assumption that Forest School has been imported wholesale from the Nordic countries, but it is not that simple. The concept of Friliuftsliv (fresh air life) is so firmly a part of the Nordic culture that being outside in wilder places is a normal part of many young children's lives, and an integral part of many settings. The cultural norm is of regular access to the outdoor environment for the majority of the population, so attitudes to the practicalities of risk-taking, campfires, knives and clothing, for example, are very different from those in the UK. Further, as early childhood education is firmly rooted in the philosophy of Froebel, with free play, creativity, socialization and emotional stability at its centre, a Forest School ethos is an integral part of everyday early years provision in the Nordic countries in a way that is not possible in most UK settings. As a kindergarten teacher in Norway in the 1970s I can attest that the culture enshrines contact with and respect for the environment in all weathers, seeing it as a spiritual and cultural issue, not just one of fostering healthy lifestyles (Henderson and Vikander 22: 2007). The Skogsmulle Foundation celebrates this idea in Sweden, aiming to raise in children a spirit of care, love and respect for nature. Thus Forest School as we know it in the UK is the transformation of an idea from one culture to another.

Forest School practitioners are drawn from a wide range of interest groups, including traditional outdoor education, traditional indoor education and different environmental disciplines. Each of these may adopt different philosophical positions when considering important questions surrounding the power of the natural environment, the nature of childhood and so on. It is therefore not surprising that there are different and strongly-held beliefs about what Forest School should be. This is good. A shared and sustainable national model for Forest School in the UK must be open to robust discussion and debate. A Special Interest Group was formed in 2004 under the umbrella of the Institute of Outdoor Learning. From this, in 2012, the independent Forest School Association (FSA) was launched to lead the establishment of Forest School as a mainstream intervention. In conjunction with the FSA, I have been researching the underlying assumptions made by different Forest School practitioners, who are working with different client groups from groups of 3- to 5-year-olds through all school ages to adults, including families (Knight 2011a). It is therefore possible for the first time to begin to explore what Forest School in the UK really is.

A definition of Forest School

The FSA has put guiding principles into its 2012 business plan, based on the research undertaken by the first development officer, and I will use these to explore the theroretical underpinnings of Forest School. The principles are as follow:

> Guiding Principles for Forest School
> 1   Forest School is a long term process with frequent and regular sessions in a local natural space, not a one-off visit. Planning, adaption, observations and reviewing are integral elements.

2 Forest School takes place in a woodland or natural wooded environment to support the development of a relationship between the learner and the natural world.

3 Forest School aims to promote the holistic development of all those involved, fostering resilient, confident, independent and creative learners.

4 Forest School offers learners the opportunity to take supported risks appropriate to the environment and themselves.

5 Forest School is run by qualified Forest School Practitioners who continuously develop their professional practice.

6 Forest School uses a range of learner centred processes to create a community for development and learning.

(Wellings 2012: 9)

1a Forest School is a long-term, regularly repeated experience

This is a key principle, separating Forest School from most other outdoor experiences. Children who participate in Forest School sessions exhibit play that is progressively deeper and more meaningful, and the benefits can be felt when they are back in their usual environments. This links with Steiner's concept of anthroposophy, natural and nature healing in communities over time (O'Brien et al. 2011). While the spiritual element of this philosophy would not be embraced by all Forest School practitioners, they concur with the links to the natural world and the emphasis that for children in their early years a 'secure, unhurried setting gives children vital social, linguistic and dexterity skills, sound foundations for emotional and cognitive intelligence' (Anthroposophy Society 2013).

The need for time, space and repetitions is like creating a pathway across a field. The first walker only dents the grass. Only by subsequent feet treading the same path will the path become permanently established. Once it has been established, then even if it falls out of use, the faint trace of its existence will be visible to archaeologists hundreds of years in the future. Ways of behaving, communicating and interacting, the enjoyment of exercise and of being in the environment are reinforced by enjoyable repetition. The Forest School experience differs from other forms of outdoor education in that its principle goal is to permanently change the participants for the good, not just to impart a one-off set of information or experiences. To do this takes time.

1b Planning, adaption, observations and reviewing are integral elements

A Forest School programme has a structure based on observations and joint working between learners and practitioners. This structure should clearly demonstrate a progression in learning and development. Basing learning opportunities on observations, adapting to the children's interests and engaging the learners with the development of opportunities is recognized good practice in many early years settings. In this way the programme is process-led, rather than outcomes-led, but has shape and progression. Because of this, early years workers often find a ready empathy with Forest School practice.

A social constructivist approach underpins the key principles of Forest School: echoing the work of Vygotsky 'with social constructivism the role of the outdoor educator or teacher is that of a facilitator who provides information and organises activities for learners to discover their own learning' (Leather 2012). Young children should be recognized as having individual interests, ideas and concerns. Inviting them to direct and control the sessions helps them to recognize their own abilities, increasing their levels of confidence and self-esteem; this is seen as a key element of good early years practice (Participation Works n.d.). The personal and autonomous nature of the learning also increases the importance of the children as stakeholders, realizing their rights in relation to their own education (Kanyal 2013).

2 Forest School takes place in a woodland or natural wooded environment

A wood or forest is the ideal setting for a Forest School session; there is something elemental and *magical* about a piece of woodland. Other wilder spaces such as beaches also have a *magic* (Knight 2011c) but Forest School is always in a forest, or a wooded area, or in a space that people aspire to become one (by planting trees or by relocating elsewhere). Woods have a significance that reverberates back to the roots of northern and western European culture, when woods covered much of the land. Sacred groves were used for religious rites, but civilization demanded cultivation and agricultural practices that destroyed the very wildness that early man had claimed as his own (Becker 2011). From earliest time there has therefore been a tension between the wild and the tamed and the role both have for healthy human existence in a healthy environment. Freudian psychology (Manning-Morton 2011) examines how the wild unconsciousness is controlled by the conscious mind, but to achieve a happy and balanced mind requires an understanding of both. Recognizing the power of wooded spaces can link to both a neo-Freudian perspective (Becker 2011) and to current thinking about the importance of developing a sense of place that creates a two-way supportive relationship between the learner and their environment (Wattchow and Brown 2011).

The importance of woods and forests has been examined by academics (e.g. Zipes 2012) looking at the cultural importance of fairy stories, many of which are set in woods (for example, Goldilocks, Red Riding Hood, Snow White, Sleeping Beauty and so on). The woods represent a strong primeval force, neither good nor evil, but a place where magic and danger can take place, a place of transformation. Zipes (2012) explores the importance of fairy tales, and within that lies the thread of the importance of forests to the development of emotional intelligence and creativity; children can feel freed to explore ideas and emotions in the secret corners of the forest spaces. Sometimes these are scary, so the availability of empathetic adults is a part of the process.

This has presented urban Forest School practitioners with a challenge, particularly in England, which is densely populated with people but less so with trees; however, private landowners and public bodies have made wooded spaces available in the centres of some of our busiest cities (Knight 2011b). For example, in London (Urbanforest 2013) and Birmingham (Brumforestschools 2013) Forest School groups are flourishing in a creative variety of spaces. Blackwell and Pound (2011) emphasize some of the different opportunities wooded spaces give to children, in contrast both to other natural spaces and to indoor spaces.

3a Forest School is about the holistic development of all those involved

To state that early years learning and development will be based on playful experiences might seem like stating the obvious, but in England the 'creep' towards more formal fact-based rote learning at ever earlier ages is a worrying trend (Brown and Patte 2013), making it essential to be clear about our methods in Forest School. Unlike children's experiences in many settings, there are few time constraints at Forest School, and no attempts to divide experiences into subject areas. Forest School is about a child-centred process of holistic development, something that seems increasingly difficult to achieve in a busy classroom or nursery, indoors or out. Isaacs described play as 'supremely the activity which brings him (sic) psychic equilibrium in the early years' (Isaacs, in Bennett et al. 1997: 3). She recognized the need for children to have time and space for making their own choices and expressing their creative spirit. Similarly Broadhead states: 'Open-ended play promotes cooperative play, with its higher cognitive challenge for interacting peers' (2004: 82). This is at the heart of Forest School and its function, which I believe is to connect children with themselves, with each other, and with their environment. Through this come the foundations for environmental awareness on which to build a sustainable lifestyle.

3b Forest School fosters resilient, confident, independent and creative learners

Forest School develops relationships and a sense of community between all participants (adults, children and young people), between the woodland and the participants, and between the 'setting' (the place that the participants have come from, such as a school, a youth club, a kindergarten) and the Forest School. Forest School leaders encourage trust and confidence on all sides. For example, most Forest Schools involve camp fires at some point. It is impossible to do this safely in the UK if trust has not been gained, as fires are no longer a cultural norm, and children may otherwise react unpredictably to them. In addition, teachers and nursery staff may be extremely nervous of fire, and need every assurance that the experience is being managed in a way appropriate to the children.

From these relationships comes creativity. Robinson (2001) identifies ways to cultivate creativity that demand time, the stimulus of trusted others, and an environment that does not demand a particular outcome. Children's response to these opportunities is often to explore their environment with increasing creative and depth; in so doing they explore the resources around them as well as their own capacities and capabilities. They also develop a sense of place and belonging, as described by Waller (2007) and Knight (2011a). A key tenet of Forest School is that participants work to find their own solutions, often to their own chosen problems, and are not constrained by the formal curriculum. Robinson (2001) talks about the function of curricula being twofold, both epistemological and managerial, and contends that the latter has come to dominate public education systems. The Cambridge Primary Review team (Alexander 2009) proposed twelve aims for primary education that chime perfectly with the educational aims of Forest School. Thus, Forest School pedagogy 'is an art form taking shape within teacher-student interaction' (Herbert 2010: 3). Tsevreni and Panayotatos (2011) have identified this style of pedagogy as a source of developing confidence and democratic learning.

4a Forest School offers learners the opportunity to take supported risks

Risks may be cognitive, emotional or physical, and will vary according to the age and experience of the participants. For example, cognitive risks may be about a willingness to get the answer wrong. Scientists and self-improvement gurus encourage adults to learn from their mistakes; experimentation at Forest School helps children to learn to accept that some techniques work better than others. Emotional risks may revolve around trust, friendships and self-expression. Forest School practitioners will work with children to develop their confidence at their own pace, knowing that for some children it can take longer than others (Elonquin and Hutchinson 2011). Physical risks are the most obvious, and the Health and Safety Executive website (HSE 2013) has extensive advice designed to reassure the nervous adult about taking children on outings into wilder spaces.

Whatever the risks are, researchers such as Gill (2010, see also Waite et al., Chapter 5, this volume) assert that it is by successfully dealing with risks that children develop necessary life skills for coping with an unpredictable world, and learn to take responsibility for their own actions. So Forest School is a 'safe enough' and not a risk-free environment.

4b 'Weather' to do Forest School – risk and weather

There is no such thing as bad weather, only bad clothing is a favourite Forest School maxim; however, this is not always accepted in England. Too often light rain showers are regarded as threatening and cold is to be avoided at all cost; many young people seem to be losing touch with the reality of how to be comfortably clothed in the outdoor environment. Without acquiring this ability it is impossible to engage positively with the environment, and to gain a sense of the changing seasons, the time of the day and the weather.

One early session was on a windy day in the rain, with grass as nearly as tall as the 4-year-old children that I was working with. One child came to tell me that she was getting wet. I agreed. When she realized that she was sanctioned to get wet, she rolled in the grass, having a new and deep experience of her environment. She developed a kinaesthetic understanding that this is what 'wet' means in relation to rain and wet grass. Similarly, in the spring of 2007 we experienced extreme cold (for England) of minus five degrees centigrade, for two sessions, and we did need to intervene to show the 5-year-old children how to increase their activity in order to increase their heat-generation, but that in itself was a deep learning experience – this is what cold feels like, and this is how we deal with it.

In an average year in the UK, sensibly-dressed children and adults can happily attend Forest School all year. By being outside in each season, the children will learn to value the difference in each, and appreciate what each contributes to our environment (Knight 2011c).

5 Forest School is run by qualified Forest School practitioners

It is a requirement of the FSA that Forest School is run by qualified Forest School practitioners. The Trainers Network, the FSA and the Forest Education Initiative work to ensure that when the training occurs under their umbrella it is rigorous in its content and delivery, to maintain the ethos and unique aspects of Forest School in the UK. As can be seen above, there are a number of elements to understand and synthesize before becoming a competent practitioner. Experts from a range of other disciplines bring valuable knowledge and skills to the training courses, but to synthesize these into a single thread of delivery practice needs training and subsequent continuing professional development.

6 Forest School uses a range of learner-centred processes to create a community for development and learning

I have stated that Forest School largely fits into a social constructivist paradigm, aiming to empower all participants to engage with the decision-making processes. For all ages, the sessions have a holistic focus, valuing skills, knowledge and the development of emotional intelligence equally. The pedagogy embraces a democratically co-constructed learning environment based on mutual trust and cooperation. There is movement in the early years sector towards giving children a voice and involving them in decision-making in settings. This reflects thinking about the benefits of early metacognition that comes from decision-making in play (Whitebread 2010: 171).

Within this environment, participants can take risks of all sorts, that are appropriate to their age and stage, and that will prepare them to be successful world citizens. The experiential learning enables them to engage with and develop a love and respect for their environment.

Forest School now, and Forest School to come?

As Forest School has become more popular, and has spread across the whole of the UK, we are seeing more and more case studies recording its benefits (for example, see those cited in Doyle and Milchem 2012). The collective evidence supports the claim that at an individual level children's physical development is encouraged, and their social, linguistic and emotional development strengthened. At a time when the UK is scoring poorly in the UNICEF studies on wellbeing (Ipsos MORI and Nairn 2011) this is important progress. These outcomes have also been linked to improvements in learning potential, but the evidence here is not as clear (Murray and O'Brien 2005). But we do know that in communities where the children are engaged in Forest School, the adults in that community are more engaged in caring for their environment, another positive outcome (Knight 2013). The FSA is actively encouraging its members to record case studies of the outcomes of Forest School for groups and individuals. Many of the training organizations also keep ethnographic references from trainees of the impact of Forest School. The Leuven scale of children's wellbeing (Laevers 1994) is a commonly used research tool, making it possible to compare group findings. Several people are pursuing PhD studies that look at the impact of Forest School and why it is so effective with all age groups, for example Burrows (2011) and McCree (2013). The weight of evidence is massing, and in time we may have sufficient robustly analysed data to support the inclusion of Forest School into the entitlement for every child.

References

Alexander, R.J. (2009) *Towards a New Primary Curriculum: A Report from the Cambridge Primary Review. Part 2: The Future.* Cambridge: University of Cambridge Faculty of Education.

Anthroposophy Society (2013) *Innovative Education Worldwide.* http://www .anthroposophy.org.uk/pages/education.php (accessed 13 June 2013).

Becker, P. (2011) Into the woods; some remarks on the cultural and biographical significance of woods and wilderness in youth work. EOE Conference Paper, Metsäkartano: http://www.seikkailukasvatus.fi/binary/file/-/id/25/fid/ 205/ (accessed 9 September 2013).

Bennett, N., Wood, L. and Rogers, S. (1997) *Teaching Through Play: Teachers' Thinking and Classroom Practice.* Buckingham: Open University Press.

Blackwell, S. and Pound, L. (2011) Forest Schools in the early years, in L. Miller, and L. Pound, (Eds) *Theories and Approaches to Learning in the Early Years.* London: Sage.

Borradaile, L. (2006) *Forest School Scotland: An Evaluation, Report to Forestry Commission Scotland and Forest Education Initiative Scotland.* Edinburgh: Forestry Commission Scotland.

Brierley, J. (1994) *Give Me a Child Until He is Seven: Brain Studies and Early Childhood Education,* 2nd edn. London: The Falmer Press.

Broadhead, P. (2004) *Early Years Play and Learning.* London: Routledge Falmer.

Brown, F. and Patte, M. (2013) *Rethinking Children's Play.* London: Bloomsbury.

Brumforestschools (2013) *Outdoor Learning in Birmingham.* http://brumforest schools.org.uk (accessed 13 October 2013).

Burrows, K. (2011) Autism, art and nature as relational aspects of Forest School, in S. Knight (ed.) *Forest School For All.* London: Sage.

Department for Education and Schools (2003) *Every Child Matters.* Annesley: DfES Publications.

Doyle, J. and Milchem, K. (2012) *Developing a Forest School in Early Years Provision.* London: Practical Pre-School Books.

Elonquin, X. and Hutchinson, T. (2011) SEALs in the woods, in S. Knight (ed.) *Forest School for All.* London: Sage.

Forest School Association (2013) *What is Forest School?* www.forestschoolassocia tion.org (accessed 13 October 2013).

Gill, T. (2010) *Nothing Ventured. . . . Balancing Risks and Benefits in the Outdoors.* Devon: English Outdoor Council. http://www.englishoutdoorcouncil.org/ wp-content/uploads/Nothing-Ventured.pdf (accessed 6 September 2013).

Henderson, B. and Vikander, N. (2007) *Nature First: Outdoor Life the Friluftsliv Way*. Toronto: Natural Heritage Books.

Herbert, A. (2010) *The Pedagogy of Creativity*. London: Routledge.

HSE (2013) *Health and Safety Executive: Education*. http://www.hse.gov.uk/services/education/index.htm (accessed 13 October 2013).

Ipsos MORI and Nairn, A. (2011) *Research in Child Wellbeing, Inequality and Materialism*. London: Ipsos MORI/ UNICEF UK.

Kanyal, M. (2013) Indian children's perceptions of their school environment, in S. Knight (ed.) *International Perspectives on Forest School*. London: Sage.

Knight, S. (2011a) Forest School as a Way of Learning in the Outdoors in the UK, *The International Journal for Cross-Disciplinary Subjects in Education (IJCDSE)*, Special Issue 1(1). http://www.infonomics-society.org/IJCDSE/Published%20papers.htm (accessed 14 January 2014).

Knight, S. (ed.) (2011b) *Forest School For All*. London: Sage.

Knight, S. (2011c) *Risk and Adventure in Early Years Outdoor Play*. London: Sage.

Knight, S. (2013) *Forest Schools and Outdoor Play in the Early Years*, 2nd edn. London: Sage.

Laevers, F. (1994) *The Leuven Involvement Scale for Young Children (LIS-YC)*. Leuven: EXE Project.

Leather, M. (2012) *Seeing the Wood from the Trees: Constructionism and Constructivism for Outdoor and Experiential Education*. Edinburgh: University of Edinburgh. http://oeandphilosophy2012.newharbour.co.uk/wp-content/uploads/2012/04/Mark-Leather.pdf (accessed 6 September 2012).

Manning-Morton, J. (2011) Not just the tip of the iceberg: psychoanalytic ideas and early years practice, in L. Miller and L. Pound (eds) *Theories and Approaches to Learning in the Early Years*. London: Sage.

McCree, M. (2013) *About Me*. http://melmccree.wordpress.com/ (accessed 12 July 2013).

Murray, R. (2003) *Forest School Evaluation Project: A Study in Wales*. London: New Economics Foundation. Report for the UK Forestry Commission. http://www.forestry.gov.uk/pdf/ForestSchoolWalesReport.pdf/$FILE/ForestSchoolWales Report.pdf (accessed 14 January 2014).

Murray, R. and O'Brien, E. (2005) *Such Enthusiasm – A Joy to See: An Evaluation of Forest School in England*. Report for the Forestry Commission. http://www.forestry.gov.uk/pdf/ForestSchoolEnglandReport.pdf/$FILE/ForestSchoolEng landReport.pdf (accessed 14 January 2014).

O'Brien, L., Burls, A., Bentsen, P. et al. (2011) Outdoor education, life long learning and skills development in woodlands and green spaces: the potential links to health and well-being, in K. Nilsson, M. Sangster, C. Gallis et al. (eds) *Forests, Trees and Human Health*, 343. DOI 10.1007/978-90-481-9806-1_12.

O'Brien, L. and Murray, R. (2006) *A Marvellous Opportunity for Children to Learn: A Participatory Evaluation of Forest School in England and Wales*. Farnham: Forest Research. http://www.forestresearch.gov.uk/fr/INFD-5Z3JVZ (accessed 6 January 2013).

O'Brien, L. and Murray, R. (2007) *Forest School and its Impacts on Young Children: Case Studies in Britain, in Urban Forestry and Urban Greening.* http://www.sciencedirect.com (accessed 2 April 2009).

Participation Works (n.d.) *Early Years.* http://www.participationworks.org.uk/topics/early-years (accessed 20 March 2013).

Robinson, K. (2001) *Out of Our Minds: Learning to be Creative.* Chichester: Capstone Publishing Ltd.

Trout, M. (2004) All about Forest Schools, *Nursery World Magazine,* 12 April.

Tsevreni, I. and Panayotatos, E. (2011) Participatory creation of a place-based teaching and learning methodology for children's participation and citizenship in the urban environment, *Children, Youth and Environments,* 21(1): 293–309. http://www.colorado.edu/journals/cye. (accessed 3 February 2013).

Urbanforest (2013) *Urban Forest Schoool at Eastwood.* http://www.urbanforestschool.co.uk (accessed 13 October 2013).

Waller, T. (2007) 'The trampoline tree and the swamp monster with 18 heads': outdoor play in the Foundation Stage and Foundation Phase, *Education 3–13,* 35(4): 393–407.

Wattchow, B. and Brown, M. (2011) *A Pedagogy of Place.* Victoria: Monash University Publishing.

Wellings, E. (2012) *Forest School National Governing Body Business Plan 2012.* Cumbria: Institute for Outdoor Learning. http://www.outdoor-learning.org/Portals/0/ForestSchoolAssociation/FS%20NGB%20FINAL%20BP%202012%5B1%5D.pdf (accessed 12 July 2012).

Whitebread, D. (2010) Play, metacognition and self-regulation, in P. Broadhead, J. Howard and E. Wood (eds) *Play and Learning in the Early Years.* London: Sage.

Yelland, N. (ed.) (2005) *Critical Issues in Early Childhood Education.* Maidenhead: Open University Press.

Zipes, J. (2012) *The Irresistible Fairy Tale: The Cultural and Social History of a Genre.* Oxford: Princeton University Press.

7 Getting the most out of outdoor spaces

Jane Waters

Introduction

This chapter offers a challenge to reflect, re-think and re-consider the 'space' in which we engage with children in order to focus on maximizing the potential of that space for children's play and learning. The Welsh context for this chapter should provide an accessible reference point for those wanting to review their pedagogic provision outside. While the discussion centres around early years classes in Wales, working under the Foundation Phase curriculum for 3–7-year-olds (DCELLS 2008), it is relevant for both school-based and non-school-based early years settings. The term 'curriculum time' is used to denote time that children are in session in early years settings in the UK, as opposed to 'playtime' and 'break-time' which, traditionally, are seen as non-curriculum-related periods of free activity where children's play outside is supervised, but not directed, by staff other than those usually designated as their teachers. The term 'teacher' is used to denote the person with designated responsibility for the learning of the children in the class, and the term 'adult' is used to denote other early years practitioners working either alongside the teacher, or in their own capacity.

In early years settings in the UK, most specifically classrooms, activity spaces are constructed for children, usually by teachers and adults, with an intended outcome in mind. While UK early years curricula include play-oriented expectations it is understood that whenever play takes place in early childhood settings it 'is shaped by the pedagogical and contextual features which surround it' (Rogers 2011: 1). With this in mind the intended outcome for a planned activity space may be play-based or goal-oriented or both. For example, a play-based outcome is intended when a role play area is set up, certain play equipment is put out or particular equipment/toys/artefacts are made available for children who then may choose to play. A goal-oriented activity may be planned with the intention of supporting, for example, children's fine motor skill development or ability to match a phonic sound to a letter shape. An activity that is both play-and goal-oriented may encourage children's playful encounters with, for example, the concepts of volume and capacity through exploration of objects in water and sand or mud areas. In these examples the teacher/adult has planned for the way in which a child may engage with the physical surroundings and for the intended outcomes of this engagement.

Despite the requirements within UK curricula documentation 'to build a curriculum on children's interests [and] to provide for learning through playful activities' (Brooker 2011: 146) children's engagement with the environment in school time will be largely in ways that have been anticipated by the teacher in the setting. Brooker's description of children being provided with 'a diet of activities dependent on specially produced learning materials with their inbuilt curriculum of colours, shapes and snap-together logic' (2011: 146) may appear bleak but may resonate with the experience of many in UK-based early years classroom settings. Clearly, children have agency: 'the capacity to act independently . . . to make choices about the things they do and to express their own ideas' (James and James 2008: 9). Children can choose to act in unexpected, unplanned or unanticipated ways but the culture of the classroom generally works to ensure compliance, over time, with a set of expected actions in specific spaces. Ailwood refers to Foucault in exploring more deeply how 'relations of power and discourses of regulation' in schools 'function to govern the everyday lives' (2011: 20) of the school community (see Ailwood 2011). Similarly, Bang explains that objects in the school environment cannot be thought of as 'neutral environmental elements' (2008: 126), since they have a functional significance, mediated by context that encourages conformity to established behaviour patterns. For example:

> The objects in the classroom contribute to the overall idea of what it means to 'go to school'. They are artefacts invented by humans . . . and they help to organise and regulate the activities of the setting. They enable the child to participate in particular activities; at the same time they serve to frame the actions of the child.
>
> (Bang 2008: 126)

When children are outside with teachers/adults, similar expectations can be established; for example, we can direct children to look, draw, measure, find, count, sort and classify. We can also set up playful encounters with materials on a larger scale than is possible indoors – tyres, rocks, logs, building blocks, boxes, pipes; we can plan for children to develop motor skills by providing ride-on equipment and the space in which to use it, by providing digging equipment and a place to dig. However, when outside we can also provide for different types of engagement between children and teachers and the environment; as Waite and Pratt explain, unfamiliar outdoor spaces can provide 'another possibility space' (2011: 8) in which the norms of interaction between teacher and child can be upset and altered, allowing for new ways of interacting.

As Maynard (2007) describes however, simply being outside, even in an unfamiliar environment, does not, of itself, alter the ways in which teachers plan for and control children's activity. In her project in which school-based teachers encountered Forest School educators with a class of children, the tensions inherent in the possibility spaces imagined by Forest School staff and those imagined by school staff were significant. Being outside can trouble the relationship that teachers have with children and so reflective engagement with the possibility space is required in order to maximize the potential of the situation.

When children are encouraged to explore and play in a natural space we cannot anticipate the outcomes of this activity with confidence since the natural space is always in a state of change, it is not fixed and can be relied upon only to be unreliable. We can be fairly sure that children will find natural outdoor spaces interesting (Heft 1988; Titman 1994; Fjørtoft 2001; Tovey 2007) and this provides the opportunity for adults to engage with children's interests (Waters and Maynard 2010; Waters 2011; Waters and Bateman 2013). This chapter seeks to provide a way of thinking about educative space that can be adopted in order to support reflective engagement on pedagogical decisions and enactment; this is particularly useful in outdoor spaces to support teachers and adults in maximizing the opportunity provided by alternative possibility spaces outdoors.

Welsh context

When the Welsh early years curriculum was in its pilot phase during 2006–8, use of outdoor space in curriculum time was the focus of attention in Welsh early years settings. A small scale study undertaken at that time indicated how teachers were tending to use outdoor spaces in ways that resembled indoor spaces and to replicate the provision and expectations found indoors (Maynard and Waters 2007). Since then there has been considerable focus on development of outdoor spaces and pedagogy, both at a policy level (e.g. DCELLS 2009) and a practice level (White 2008; Bilton 2010, see also Maynard, Chapter 4 this volume). To date there has been no large-scale empirical work to explore whether the pedagogical approaches adopted in outdoor spaces in Wales maximize the potential for children's learning therein; however, the Welsh Government have established an evaluation of the Foundation Phase that is due to report in 2014/15.

Across Wales there is considerable variation in practice (see Estyn 2011; Maynard et al. 2013), but most settings in Wales offer some outdoor access and experience for children in curriculum time at least for Nursery (age 3–4 years old) and Reception (age 4–5 years old) classes and most usually for Year 1 and Year 2 classes (ages 5–6 and 6–7 years old respectively). Teachers/adults have different approaches to where they position themselves during curriculum time, which could be spent outside or inside. For example, teachers may choose to be outside directing children's activity to support specific learning in a planned goal-oriented task; they may choose to place themselves outside to join children's playful engagement with the environment; they may choose to position themselves indoors to scaffold learning in goal-oriented tasks with some children while other children play outside; or they may position themselves indoors in order to join in with children's playful activity indoors.

Whatever the approach adopted, and, of course, this approach may vary from day to day, there will be some purpose to children's outdoor activity in curriculum time. This chapter explores how we can evaluate activity in different spaces and support the kind of activity we want in order to get the best outcomes for children during their curriculum time outdoors.

Affordance

The concept of affordance is frequently adopted by those interested in children's use of outdoor space. This notion can relate to any interaction between an individual and an environment – indoors or outdoors – but it is particularly useful as a means of thinking about what spaces offer to children. Affordance is a term that was 'made up' by Gibson (1979: 127) to describe the 'complementarity' (1979: 127) between an environment and an individual within it. Unlike a physical feature such as height, colour or shape the affordance of the environment for the individual is not fixed or located within the environment, it is located *between* the individual and the environment – in the individual's perception of what the environment offers them. When we think about this in terms of what a space offers a child, the affordance of the space is what the child perceives they are able to do there.

Gibson's work allows us to understand that when children encounter a physical space they perceive what can be done there; they perceive the affordances available to them in the space:

> The fact that a stone is a missile does not imply that it cannot be other things as well. It can be a paperweight, a bookend, a hammer, or a pendulum bob. It can be piled on other rocks to make a cairn or a stone wall. These affordances are all consistent with one another. The differences between them are not clear cut, and the arbitrary names by which they are called do not count for perception. If you know what can be done with a graspable detached object, what it can be used for, you can call it whatever you please.
>
> (Gibson 1979: 134)

A child encountering a field containing a fallen branch does not simply mentally categorize *field, branch* but recognizes runable, jumpable (see Figure 7.1).

Figure 7.1   Child (6) in parkland during school visit.

While Gibson was interested in human visual perception of the physical features of a space, others have developed his theory (e.g. Heft 1988; Kyttä 2004; Waters 2011) to include consideration of the sociocultural features of a space and their relation to what takes place within it. In terms of the affordance of a space for a child this helps us understand the importance of what the child perceives they are allowed/encouraged to do in the space. It is important here to recall the discussion above referring to the mediating context, discourse(s) and power relations that shape activity in any space.

A tree is climbable if it has low enough branches for the child to reach but this affordance is not present if the accompanying adult has imposed a 'no climbing' rule that day, or indeed the child's parents/carers have a long-standing rule that clothes and shoes must be looked after and should not be spoiled or dirtied. For a child who does not enjoy or choose to climb, the affordance *climbable* may not be perceived; instead, if a camera is available, the affordance *photographable* may take precedence. We cannot assume that we can define what affordances exist within different spaces on behalf of another individual (adult or child). We can use Gibson's work to help us reflect upon and understand what does happen in the different spaces that we provide for children and how we might influence activity in a space in future.

When we consider children's activity in a space there are three aspects to think about as shown in Figure 7.2.

Individual activity references the child's agency. As an autonomous individual, each child will perceive different opportunities for action and interaction within a space and will make choices about their engagement with activity whether this is directed or self-initiated.

The **physical** aspect of the space refers to what, and who, is present. The physical features, objects and people in the space provide multiple and varied opportunities for interaction, which may or may not include verbal language. Bang reminds us that objects in a space carry meaning that is tied to the context (2008); the context of a teacher being present may alter the meaning of any object in the space.

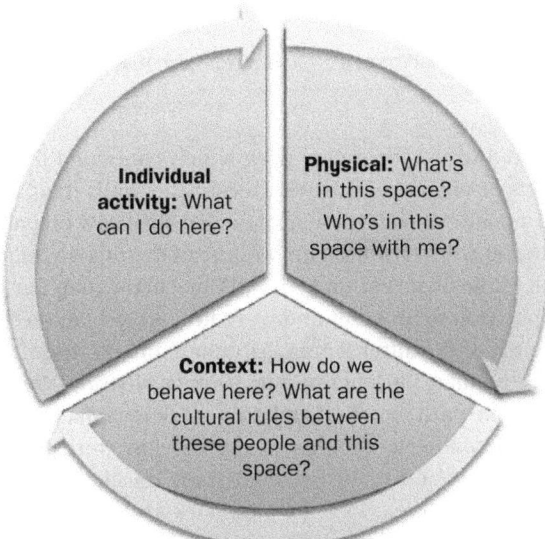

Figure 7.2 Individual, physical and contextual aspects of a space (see also Waters 2013).

The **contextual** aspect of the space refers to the socioculturally agreed norms of activity within the space. In school settings this includes rules about behaviour, noise, permission to talk – about what and to whom; rights to touch – what and when; and expectations about accepted interactional patterns between, for example, adults and children. Waite and Pratt refer to this as the 'micro-culture of a particular learning space' (2011: 7).

By considering these aspects when we review children's activity in a space, we can begin to understand what may restrict or support aspects of behaviour, interaction and learning within the space. It is then that we can consider how to best support the outcomes we intend for any particular situation.

Case studies

Consider the following two case studies in which two early years classes from the same school undertake off-site visits to the same geographic area (containing a local community play-park and a wilder, natural country park) in the same week.

Each class visited the off-site locality once a month with the support of volunteer students who brought the adult:child ratio to 1:2/3. A risk assessment visit was made by a staff member on the day of the visit to ensure that there were no significant dangers in the locality.

Observation 1: Class A

A mixed Year 1/2 class of 27 children (15 Year 1 and 12 Year 2)

Teacher: Sam

The children walked to the local play-park which contained fixed play equipment and an area of shrubs and trees. During the walk they were asked to record any road signage and street markings that they saw on paper clipped to a clipboard that they were to hold. This walk usually took 15 minutes but took longer as a result of the observation activity. Once in the play-park the children handed their clipboards to an adult and were invited to play on the equipment or in a specified part of the natural area. After half an hour the class walked for five minutes to the country park in order to access a clearing, that was a further five minutes along the path, where they had a drink and snack.

For Sam, the intended outcomes of the session were that the children would notice, recognize and record road signage during the road walk. Sam intended for the children to explore the play-park area and express interest in the natural area of shrubs and trees. The walk to the country park for a drink and snack was to provide a relaxing end to the trip.

During this session there were no interactions involving sustained or shared thinking between adults and children. Talk that involved adult to child direction was high, particularly during the walk to the play-park and having left it. Child to child talk was high. Child to adult talk was low.

Sam, on reflection following the trip, expressed disappointment that the children had required a high level of management when outside in order to keep them on task with the observational activity. She was again disappointed that the children chose only to climb on the play equipment and run around a bush in the natural area of the local play-park. Sam expressed concern about children's safety when in the country park, explaining that local youths and dog walkers use the area and there may be dangerous or inappropriate objects (for example, needles and condoms) as well as dog faeces on the ground.

Observation 2: Class B

A mixed Year 1/2 class of 26 children (8 Year 1 and 18 Year 2)

Teacher: Ella

The session involved a 20-minute walk to the country park during which time the children talked to each other, with some conversational interaction between teacher/adults and children. In places children and the teacher/adults pointed out features of interest – cars, houses belonging to family members, locations of recalled events (e.g. bike ride, walk with grandparents). Once in the country park, the children asked if the whole group could go 'off the path' to access the higher ground more quickly. The group then spent half an hour ensuring everyone reached the top of a steep slope. During this time interactions between adults and children were focused on how to solve the problem of getting up the slope; some interactions were sustained and involved shared thinking in which children contributed to the solution and positive outcome. Talk involving adult to child direction was low. Child to child talk was high. Child to adult talk was high.

Once the whole group had reached the top some children began singing and the rest joined in. The remainder of the session in the country park involved children's playful activity and exploration of the area to which they had climbed.

For Ella, the intended outcomes for this session were related to children being able to express themselves to each other and to the adults, demonstrating interest in their local environment. She also intended that the children work together to explore, play and/or problem solve in the natural space of the country park as the opportunity arose.

Ella, on reflection following the trip, expressed amazement at the children's request to climb the steep path and was very pleased with the way in which the children and adults had helped each other work out how to ensure everyone got to the top successfully. She stated that the spontaneous song when this was achieved was a moment of 'pure magic' and she would treasure the memory.

When interviewed at a later date and asked to recall highlights of her year with the class Ella made specific reference to this event, and added that the children often referred to it in school; it had become a shared and celebrated event for the class.

Reflection

When we consider these two events using the model based on affordance theory (Figure 7.2 above and Table 7.1 below) we can review children's activity in the light of the three aspects of the space; this helps us understand why the children's experiences were so different and why the satisfaction of the teachers was also so different. We also see that in order to fully review children's engagement with outdoor spaces we must consider a number of interweaving aspects of the space (including our own pedagogy) in a manner that engages honestly with the sociocultural features of the early years setting.

At first, it appears fairly straightforward to understand Ella's satisfaction with class B's experience. She had intended that the children enjoy the event and that they lead the activity in which they would be engaged. Her learning goals were related to children being able to express themselves, demonstrate interest in their local environment and that they work together to explore, play and/or problem solve in the natural space of the country park as the

Table 7.1 Summary of the aspects of the outdoor space for each class in the case study

	Class A	Class B
Physical aspects of the space	**What was there**? Urban roads, play-park including standard fixed play equipment and a small area planted with shrubs with interweaving pathways; wild natural space in the country park including a defined pathway **Who was there**? Other children and accompanying adults, teacher	**What was there**? Urban roads, wild natural space in the country park including a defined pathway **Who was there**? Other children and accompanying adults, teacher
Contextual aspects of the space	Goal-directed observation activity established for the road walk involving use of clipboards The local play-park was often accessed by children out of school time The teacher described the time in the play-park as 'playtime'. The adults sat/stood and watched children's activity in the play-park Warnings were issued about the possible hazards in the country park. The children were directed to walk on the path and sit down to have their drink and snack in a defined space	There was no direction to undertake specific activity during the road walk; the teacher/adults talked conversationally with children The children had accessed the country park in the past for exploratory child-led sessions of activity
Individual children's activity	Some children engaged with the observation task, many children did not unless asked a specific question directly by an adult Most children chose to climb on the play equipment in the play-park; a few left this area after a short while to chase each other around the shrubs in the natural area using the defined pathways	During the road walk the children drew each other's and the adults'/teacher's attention to aspects of interest in the environment On entry to the country park two children made a request to climb a steep slope; most of the other children repeated this request after hearing it expressed

Table 7.1 Summary of the aspects of the outdoor space for each class in the case study (*continued*)

Class A	Class B
All the children walked along the path in the country park, and sat down as directed for refreshments	The children and adults negotiated how to ensure everyone could climb the slope successfully One child started singing and the other children joined in as the last of them reached the top of the slope Children explored the country park, collecting, talking about and playing with loose parts and features therein

opportunity arose; however, the achievement of these goals was supported by the three aspects of the space:

Physically, the environment offered a stimulus to which the children responded positively, both the familiar urban landmarks of the road walk and the topological features of the country park afforded children the opportunity for stimulation and interest (see also Waters and Maynard 2010). The fact that the teacher walked with the children (not at the front or the back) and that there were enough adults to supervise as well as provide conversational talk partners afforded the verbal expression of the children's interest to the adults as well as each other.

Contextually, there were few rules, (other than safety rules, e.g. walking on the pavement and not on the road, staying in sight of others in the country park); the teacher and adults made themselves available for conversation and purposely did not direct activity. They had explicitly planned in advance that they would respond to children's interests and support self-expression. The teacher, adults and children were confident users of the country park, having made at least four previous visits, and were aware of, but not worried by, possible hazards.

Children understood that in this activity they could express themselves freely and make suggestions; they trusted the teacher and adults to listen to them. They engaged in conversation with each other and the teacher and adults present during the walk to the country park and then engaged with a challenging opportunity presented by the physical features of the country park. The children expressed pride and achievement in meeting the challenge by singing when they had completed it.

Sam, on the other hand, expressed disappointment with her class's experience. She had intended that the children recognize and note down road signs and signs that give instructions to drivers/pedestrians along the road walk. She had provided observation sheets on clipboards for the children to use to record what they saw. Sam wanted the children to engage with the park area in an exploratory manner, particularly the natural shrubby area that was on a slight slope and contained a number of objects of interest – seeds, tree roots, natural small parts and a muddy area. It was here, rather than in the country park, that she hoped the children would express interest in the natural environment. Sam intended the country park to be a quiet and peaceful place for the children to enjoy their drink and snack before returning to the school. She did not plan for any particular outcomes associated with this last part of the afternoon, other than a relaxing walk with informal interaction between adults and children. When we consider Sam's disappointment we can similarly think about each aspect of the space:

Physically, the environment offered features in which children might have shown an interest (see Titman 1994; Waters and Maynard 2010) both during the road walk, in the play-park and the country park. The teacher, other adults and children were present though generally the children chose only to interact with each other. The children were holding clipboards which may have hindered physical interaction with small, found objects during the road walk.

Contextually, the road walk had been organized as a directed activity. The children were given a task by the teacher and expected to undertake it. The task-based activity was monitored and promoted above other types of activity. The clipboard represented the directed nature of the task and, if we accept Bang's assertion about objects representing relationships of power (2008), may have indicated that the adult–child relationship during the walk was as 'teacher' and 'taught'. The road was familiar to the children; they had walked it before in school time and, most frequently, in their own time. Whereas the children in Ella's class drew attention to aspects of the familiar road walk with each other and the adults, such activity in Sam's class was regulated and disallowed because the purpose of the walk was to notice and record signage. The 'rules of the space' then in these two classes were very different. Once Sam's class reached the play-park Sam indicated the end of the directed activity by asking children to give their clipboards in and explaining that they could now play in the park, on the equipment or in the natural area up the slope. Arguably the 'rules of the space' at this time were similar to playtime in school: the adults observed children, monitoring safety and behaviour and did not proactively engage with them. That the children engaged with the space in a way that was reminiscent of their activity in a school playtime is therefore unsurprising. They did not engage in an exploratory manner with the natural space since to so do would run counter to the expectation of behaviour at playtime; indeed the opportunity for exploration may not even have been perceived. When the children were directed to stop playing and walk to the country park for their drink and snack this transition was reminiscent of the end of playtime, the 'rules of the space' again reflecting a teacher-directed activity.

Children in class A generally chose not to engage with the observation task during the road walk. They tended to talk among themselves and record signage when directed or invited to do so by an adult. When in the park the children played on the play equipment – a familiar activity in this park – and ran around the natural area. While the physical space may have afforded exploratory natural-world play the children engaged in behaviour such as running and chasing, typical of 'playtime' at school, in this space. Once directed to walk to the country park the children chose to comply with instructions related to drink and snack organization and to limitations imposed by the hazards of the space perceived by the teacher.

Discussion

For Sam's class, A, the 'fit' between the intended outcomes and the three aspects of space was limited. First the children responded without enthusiasm to the observation task; the fact that the children were mobile in a noisy environment in which it was tricky to balance a clipboard in order to record information meant that adults were highly directive for this part of the outdoor session. The pedagogic approach was representative of a directed session indoors, despite taking place in an environment that did not support quiet or concentrated attention to the task. Second, on entering the play-park Sam expected the children to explore and express their interest in what she hoped they would find a stimulating natural space. However, they responded as if it was 'playtime' in school. They were not supported by the context in perceiving other affordances in that space, arguably because the context of the visit was reflective of a school session followed by playtime. The children were compliant with the teacher's direction for the brief walk to the country park; however, they did not engage in conversation with the adults as Sam had hoped, possibly because the cultural context of the visit disallowed such informality and the reiteration of the hazards of the space discouraged engagement with it in the presence of (regulatory) adults. Though the children had visited the country park previously it was usually under similar circumstances; if they perceived opportunities for engagement, challenge and interest in this space then they did not share this with the adults since to do so would run counter to the 'rules of the space'. This is in contrast to the experience in Ella's class where the 'fit' between the intended outcomes and the three aspects of space was good. Here it is worth reiterating that Ella's pedagogic approach during her outdoor trip was explicitly to hear children's views, to listen and engage with their interests and ideas. She did not therefore direct activity other than for safety reasons, and the supporting adults behaved in similar fashion, following her lead. Ella's pedagogic approach, then, created a cultural context that supported the aims of the activity. The three aspects of the space were in harmony with her intended outcomes. Sam had adopted a directive pedagogic approach for the first part of the visit and it is possible that this had 'set the scene' for the interactions that followed. Sam's pedagogic approach, and the associated cultural context, was therefore at odds with the intended aims of the play-park-based part of the visit. The three aspects of the space did not support the aims of the activity.

The purpose of the case studies above is to emphasize that, in provision of outdoor spaces for children's learning, we must consider and plan for a coherent match between the physical and contextual aspects of a space and the pedagogical approach taken, in order to best support children's individual choices in the space. The affordance of a space for children's learning is supported *or limited* by the cultural context – the 'rules of the space' – as well as by what, and who, is physically available. If we want to encourage children to engage meaningfully with outdoor environments we must ensure that our pedagogic approach creates the appropriate cultural climate for them to do so. By reflecting on children's activity using the three-aspect model practitioners are empowered to make changes to support the kinds of activity they want children to engage in when they are outside in curriculum time.

References

Ailwood, J. (2011) It's about power: researching play, pedagogy and participation in the early years of school, in S. Rogers (ed.) *Rethinking Play and Pedagogy in Early Childhood Education.* Abingdon: Routledge.

Bang, J. (2008) Conceptualising the environment of the child in a cultural-historical approach, in M. Hedegaard and M. Fleer (eds) *Studying Children: A Cultural-Historical Approach.* Maidenhead: McGraw-Hill Education.

Bilton, H. (2010) *Outdoor Learning in the Early Years.* London: Routledge.

Brooker, L. (2011) Taking children seriously: an alternative agenda for research? *Journal of Early Childhood Research*, 9(2): 137–49.

DCELLS (2008) *Foundation Phase Framework for Children's Learning for 3–7 year olds in Wales.* Cardiff: Welsh Assembly Government.

DCELLS (2009) *The Outdoor Learning Handbook.* Cardiff: Welsh Assembly Government.

Estyn (2011) *Outdoor Learning: An Evaluation of Learning in the Outdoors for Children Under 5 in the Foundation Phase.* Cardiff: Estyn.

Fjørtoft, I. (2001) The natural environment as a playground for children: the impact of outdoor play activities in pre-primary school children, *Early Education Journal*, 29(2): 111–17.

Gibson, J.J. (1979) *The Ecological Approach to Visual Perception.* London: Lowrence Erlbanm.

Heft, H. (1988) Affordances of children's environments: a functional approach to environmental description. *Children's Environments Quarterly*, 5(3): 29–37.

James, A. and James, A. (2008) *Key Concepts in Childhood Studies*. London: Sage.

Kyttä, M. (2004) The extent of children's independent mobility and the number of actualized affordances as criteria for child-friendly environments, *Journal of Environmental Psychology*, 24: 179–98.

Maynard, T. (2007) Encounters with Forest School and Foucault: a risky business? *Education 3–13*, 35(4): 379–91.

Maynard. T., Taylor, C., Waldron, S. et al. (2013) *Evaluating the Foundation Phase: Policy Logic Model and Programme Theory*. Cardiff: Welsh Government Social Research.

Maynard, T. and Waters, J. (2007) Learning in the outdoor environment: a missed opportunity? *Early Years*, 27(3): 255–65.

Rogers, S. (ed.) (2011) *Rethinking Play and Pedagogy in Early Childhood Education*. Abingdon: Routledge.

Titman, W. (1994) *Special Places, Special People: The Hidden Curriculum of School Grounds*. Godalming: World Wide Fund for Nature/Learning through Landscapes.

Tovey, H. (2007) *Playing Outdoors: Spaces and Places, Risk and Challenge*. Maidenhead: Open University Press.

Waite, S. and Pratt, N. (2011) Theoretical perspectives on learning outside the classroom: relationships between learning and place, in S. Waite (ed.) *Children Learning Outside the Classroom: From Birth to Eleven*. London: Sage.

Waters, J. (2011) A sociocultural consideration of child-initiated interaction with teachers in indoor and outdoor spaces. Unpublished PhD thesis, Swansea University.

Waters, J. (2013) Talking in wild outdoor spaces: children bringing their interests to their teachers, in S. Knight (ed.) *International Perspectives on Forest School: Natural Spaces to Play and Learn*. London: Sage.

Waters, J. and Bateman, A. (2013) Revealing the interactional features of learning and teaching moments in outdoor activity, *European Early Childhood Education Research Journal*, doi:10.1080/1350293X.2013.798099

Waters, J. and Maynard, T. (2010) What elements of the natural outdoor environment do children of 4–7 years attend to in their child-initiated interactions with teachers? *European Early Childhood Education Research Journal Special Edition*, 18(4): 473–83.

White, J. (2008) *Playing and Learning Outdoors: Making Provision for High-Quality Experiences in the Outdoor Environment*. Abingdon: Routledge.

Section 3

International perspectives

8 Early years outdoor play in Scandinavia

Ellen Beate Hansen Sandseter

Background

Scandinavia consists of three countries: Denmark, Sweden and Norway. These three countries lie in the northern part of Europe with a relatively cold climate, although there is great variation between the different seasons of the year. The winters are quite cold and snowy in the northern parts of Scandinavia, while there is a milder climate in the southern parts where winters are more wet than snowy. The coastal regions also usually have milder winters than the inland. The summer climate also varies a great deal, and while Denmark and the southern parts of Sweden and Norway have quite warm and stable temperatures during summer, the northern parts are colder.

The population in the Scandinavian countries ranges from 9.6 million inhabitants in Sweden, 5.5 million in Denmark and 5 million in Norway. Denmark is quite a small country in terms of land area with its 45,000 square kilometres, while Norway and Sweden are around 450,000–500,000 square metres. Still, the population density is quite low in Scandinavia with 126 people per square kilometre in Denmark, 21 in Sweden and 13 in Norway. The terrain in the Scandinavian countries includes a lot of mountains in the northern parts, especially on the west coast of Norway, and more flat landscapes in the southern parts and especially in Denmark. Still, all three Scandinavian countries have a large proportion of forest and wild natural environments with easy access for most of their inhabitants, and all three countries have a 'law of common access' (or similar) which gives the citizens free access to uncultivated land and the right to walk and stay in nature areas, such as woodland, mountain areas, by the seashore, by rivers etc., even though it is in private ownership.

Early childhood education and care policy in Scandinavia

In all three Scandinavian countries early childhood education and care (ECEC) is placed within the wider educational system as a part of lifelong learning. ECEC is not statutory for children in Scandinavia, but all three countries have laws that secure all children the right to be offered a place in an ECEC setting in the years before they reach school age (up to 6 years in Norway and Denmark and up to 7 years in Sweden). Because of this right most of all children in these countries attend ECEC; 84 per cent of all 1- to 5-year-olds in Sweden, 97 per cent of all 3- to 5-year-olds and 67 per cent of all birth to 2-year-olds in Denmark, and 97 per cent of all 3- to 5-year-olds and 80 per cent of all 1- to 2-year-olds in Norway.

Scandinavian ECEC is considered to be of high quality and associated with positive outcomes for children and families (Barnados and Start Strong 2012). These outcomes are also associated with the high level of welfare and economic resources in Scandinavia and the low levels of poverty rates; however, Scandinavian ECEC was also built on basic values and traditions that still characterize the ECEC provision in Norway, Sweden and Denmark today.

Scandinavian nations emphasize the holistic development of children as the focus for work in ECEC institutions. All three countries have a law regarding ECEC stating that the primary aim of the provision is to facilitate the wellbeing, health, development and learning of children (the Norwegian Ministry of Education and Research (NMER) 2005; the Danish Ministry of Social Affairs and Integration (DMSI) 2011; the Swedish Ministry of Education and Science (SMES) 1985). According to each of the countries' ECEC curriculum, ECEC work is commonly based on values such as child participation, democracy, human rights, play, social relationships, respect for nature, sustainability and individual needs (NMER 2006/2011, SMES 2010, The Danish parliament (DP) 2004). Children's wellbeing in Scandinavian ECEC is closely related to their right to participate and based on democratic values (Borge et al. 2003; Nilsen 2008; Aasen et al. 2009; Sandberg and Ärlemalm-Hagsér 2011). In practice, children should be viewed as active meaning-makers with regard to their own lives. Therefore, children in Scandinavian ECEC institutions have the right to express their views concerning their day-to-day activities and should regularly be provided the opportunity to take an active part in planning and assessing the activities of the setting. In the Norwegian curriculum, this viewpoint is expressed thus: 'Children's views shall be given due weight according to their age and maturity' (NMER 2006/2011). In practice, children should have a significant degree of freedom with regard to choosing their activities and where they spend their time. 'All children in kindergarten should be given the opportunity to play what they like, but the staff can initiate other kinds of play if the child repeats a narrow range of play types' (Norwegian preschool teacher, 27.10.09).

Although Scandinavian ECEC has a child-centered pedagogy and largely emphasizes children's freedom, a plan exists for their development and learning. All curricula plans state that ECEC institutions must be goal oriented and develop their own plans to attain the aims of the curriculum. The Norwegian curriculum includes seven knowledge areas that guide the pedagogical work in ECEC institutions: communication; language and text; body, movement and health; art, culture and creativity; nature, environment and technology; ethics, religion and philosophy; local community and society; and number, spaces and shapes (NMER 2006/2011). The Danish curriculum uses six major themes upon which the ECEC settings focus their work: children's diverse personal development; social competence; language; body and movement; nature and nature phenomenon; and cultural expressions and values (DP 2004). In the Swedish curriculum particular knowledge areas are not outlined; however, the aims of the ECEC provision are described by focusing on norms (democracy and solidarity), development (e.g., social, motor, literacy, mathematic, aesthetic and cultural development) and children's participation/influence (SMES 2010). Nevertheless, the professional approach to children's learning in ECEC should be through play (Aasen et al. 2009; Sandberg and Ärlemalm-Hagsér 2011). According to this view, play has an intrinsic value and is part of a child's culture.

> In this kindergarten, the emphasis is on free play. This is because we acknowledge the quality of this kind of play, and experience that children learn and develop through this play. They gain skills within the seven knowledge areas in the Framework Plan and more general social and relational skills through free play. . . This means arranging for situational learning here and now. It does not have to be organized by the staff; rather, it includes the importance of the staff being flexible and attentive to children's interests. For instance, the flexibility to stop while on a hike in the forest because some children have discovered something that caught their interest: a spider, a worm, some trees, etc. In this way, the children continuously learn, guided by their own motivation. It is not a question of IF children learn; it's just a question of what and when children learn. In our opinion, the children learn best when their own curiosity and motivation is the basis.
>
> (Norwegian preschool teacher, 27.10.09)

Play is regarded as a phenomenon with instrumental value and a means for learning and developing a complex set of skills involving both expressions and impressions. Socially, play serves an opportunity for developing social competence and gaining knowledge and insight in many areas (NMER 2006/2011). Generally, play as a phenomenon is looked upon as a way of learning in different knowledge areas.

Outdoor play

One of the important values in Scandinavian ECEC is the acknowledgement of outdoor play and outdoor life as an important part of children's lives. In Scandinavian societies, the concept of *friluftsliv* (which is similar to the concept of 'outdoor life', but with stronger connotations of values and lifestyle) is an important part of the regional cultural heritage. The traditions of visiting nature areas, hiking in mountainous or forest areas, sleeping out in the wild, fishing, hunting and exploring have been maintained over generations as a part of daily life (Borge et al. 2003; Ärlemalm-Hagsér 2008; Aasen et al. 2009; Ejbye-Ernst 2012). Furthermore, many Scandinavians habitually travel to parks, playgrounds and nature areas for hiking and recreation in their spare time with family and friends (Borge et al. 2003; Nilsen 2008). This cultural heritage is also included in the ECEC system as an important foundation upon which the content and practices of ECEC institutions are based.

The Scandinavian ECEC curricula all emphasize outdoor play and experiences in natural environments as vital for children's wellbeing, development and learning. In the Norwegian curriculum (NMER 2006/2011: 16) outdoor play is particularly emphasized: 'Outdoor play and activities are an important part of child culture that must be retained, regardless of the geographic and climatic conditions.' Similarly, the Swedish curriculum states that 'outdoor life should give [children] opportunities for play and activities both in designed environments and in natural environments . . . [and that] ECEC institutions shall have a strong emphasis on environmental questions and sustainability of nature' (SMES 2010: 7). The Danish curriculum handbook (Kjær and Olesen 2005: 12) also strongly emphasizes the same theme through statements such as: 'Children in ECEC institutions shall have the opportunity to experience the joy of spending time in nature in different seasons, and they shall develop a respect for nature and environment.'

The Norwegian white paper regarding outdoor life (friluftsliv; NME 2000–2001) places a great responsibility upon all ECEC providers and schools to use outdoor life as an important part of rearing Norwegian children. Nilsen (2008) suggested that this responsibility might be a way in which policy is being used to ensure that Norwegian traditions are continued among the younger generations during a time when there is a worry that these traditions will decline due to the new activities and sports available for young people. Another discussion in Norway concerns the idea that nature and outdoor ECEC are just modern forms of Froebel's original concept of Kindergarten: gardens *for* children in which children learn and develop by being in the centre of things and acting in the physical world (i.e. the garden; Borge et al. 2003). Nevertheless, the Scandinavian outdoor ECEC is solidly rooted in the beliefs of politicians, practitioners and parents that children are happy when playing outside (Borge et al. 2003; Ärlemalm-Hagsér 2008; Ejbye-Ernst 2012).

In Scandinavian ECEC settings, being outdoors is closely related to non-organized play and exploration. The fundamental approach of Scandinavian ECEC settings is that children are naturally curious, and they explore their world and capabilities using their whole bodies. In this sense, the physical environment is important during this phase of life to ensure that children have a wide range of experiences across formal and informal learning situations. Scandinavian ECEC in general, and Norwegian ECEC in particular, expect learning and development to change within an individual's resource system as a result of encountering and mastering challenges and not due to the increasing maturity associated with age (Hendry and Kloep 2002). In addition, the Gibsonian approach (later revised by Heft 1988 and Kyttä 2006) has a strong standing in Norwegian ECEC. The idea of *affordances*, features of the environment that allow an individual to perform particular actions, is central to Gibsonian theory; however, the individual must explore to learn about the many affordances in their environments (Gibson 1988). Therefore, Gibsonian theory emphasizes direct engagement with the environment in order to learn about what the environment offers. Transmission of information via other methods (e.g. verbal or pictorial) is not adequate. Opportunities for exploration will be central to the pedagogy of practitioners working directly from Gibsonian theory or extensions of Gibsonian theory (e.g. Heft 1988 and Kyttä 2006). This method will lead to a greater emphasis of the physical environment and a direct relationship between the environment and learning (Sandseter et al. 2012).

Outdoor preschools

Although Scandinavian ECEC commonly focuses on outdoor education, an increasing trend also exists for an outdoor ECEC provision via so-called 'outdoor preschools' with a particularly strong focus on outdoor play and learning (Lysklett 2013). These ECEC settings are growing in number.

Denmark was the first Scandinavian country to establish ECEC institutions that focused on outdoor life and hiking. These first settings emerged as early as (approximately) 1950, although the first Danish 'Skovbørnehave' (Forest kindergartens) settings, as we know them today, were established in 1985 (Ejbye-Ernst, 2012). Today, Denmark has more than five hundred such ECEC settings. Outdoor preschools in Denmark were developed because outdoor provision was considered to be beneficial for child development and learning, but also as a result of the need to offer more Danish children a place for ECEC in the early 1980s (Eilers 2005).

Likewise, early versions of outdoor preschools existed in Norway in the late 1940s, when the motto was to locate children 'up in the heights and out in nature' (Lysklett 2013). Nevertheless, the modern outdoor preschools first appeared in the late 1980s. These sites were somewhat inspired by the Danish Skovbørnehave as well as strongly based on the Norwegian cultural tradition of having a close relationship with nature and outdoor life and the notion that being outdoors and in close contact with nature is beneficial for child development and wellbeing (Borge et al. 2003). The actual number of outdoor preschools in Norway is not known due to the difficulties of counting them (i.e. a governmental definition or register of such settings does not exist). Nevertheless, estimations indicate that more than four hundred sites existed in 2005 and 2006, and one might presume that even more exist today (Ejbye-Ernst 2012).

In addition, Sweden's first outdoor preschool was established in 1985. In Sweden, these settings are called 'I ur och skur-førskola' (outdoor preschool) (Drougge et al. 2007; Änggård 2012). Today, more than two hundred outdoor settings are found in Sweden (Änggård 2012; Ejbye-Ernst 2012). The development of these Swedish outdoor settings was based on the idea that children's desire for knowledge, physical activity and social relationships are better met in natural rather than indoor environments (Änggård 2012). Sweden has also strongly focused on children's understanding and knowledge of nature as well as sustainable development as a part of ECEC, particularly in outdoor preschools (Drougge et al. 2007; Ärlemalm-Hagsér 2008; Änggård 2012).

Thus, approximately 5–10 per cent of all Scandinavian ECEC settings are outdoor preschools (although even more might exist due to the difficulties of defining this type of ECEC and the fact that these settings are autonomous with regard to their pedagogical profile and what they choose to call themselves).

Outdoor preschools typically emphasize natural environments as a space for their pedagogical practice and work. Furthermore, they focus on actively using the diverse and changing features of nature, across seasons and climates, throughout the year, as their way of working with the curriculum content (Lysklett et al. 2003; Drougge et al. 2007; Ejbye-Ernst 2012). Children in outdoor preschools in Scandinavia usually spend five to seven hours outdoors in diverse environments (Borge et al. 2003). The pedagogical arguments for such provision are that children gain knowledge and understanding from their close contact with nature and their activities in diverse nature environments and that knowledge about the local natural and cultural environment is an important factor to preserve one's cultural heritage. In addition, research show that children develop motor and physical skills by encountering challenges in natural environments (Grahn et al. 1997; Fjørtoft 2000; Fiskum 2004).

Although Scandinavia has a relatively large proportion of outdoor preschools, children in all types of ECEC settings spend a large portion of their day outdoors, often between 30 and 70 per cent of their time (Mårtensson 2004; Moser and Martinsen 2010; Ejbye-Ernst 2012). From an international perspective, then, all Scandinavian ECEC settings might be regarded as outdoor preschools.

Outdoor spaces

Outdoor playgrounds in Scandinavian ECEC settings are usually designed with standardized equipment similar to those of many other Western countries. Swings, slides, sandpits, walls for climbing, boats for playing in and other items designed for children's play are commonly found. Although these standardized playgrounds might resemble the ECEC playgrounds of England, Australia, America and other countries, the ECEC playgrounds in Scandinavia are, to some extent, larger, more varied and include more natural features. A comparison between Norway and Australia revealed that while Australian ECEC playgrounds had an average of 7 m^2 per child, Norway had an average of 55 m^2 per child, and Norwegian ECEC practitioners evaluated their ECEC play environments as much more varied and stimulating for children than their Australian counterparts (Little et al. 2012). Having larger and more stimulating outdoor ECEC playgrounds might make spending more time outdoors for play and learning easier and more attractive for both children and practitioners. More space also affords children more opportunities for varied play, activity and experiences.

In addition, many children in Scandinavian ECEC settings spend a significant amount of time in other and more natural environments and often make their own campsites in local nature areas during regular visits. Children usually have access to the wild landscape of the neighbouring areas, which also provides multiple opportunities for free play and learning situations.

Children in Scandinavian ECEC are, as already mentioned, given the opportunity to access their play environment with great independence and freedom and to utilize the environment to create play and activities based on their own initiative. This ability to move freely, children's *independent mobility licence*, is an important factor that enables free action and meets their desire to escape adult control; thus, this factor is closely linked to the ability to optimally use their play environment (Kyttä 2004). Within a Gibsonian approach where a direct relationship between the environment and learning is the basis, both the child's opportunity to move freely and the environment is of great importance (Sandseter et al. 2012).

Several researchers have studied and discussed the effect of the outdoor environment on children's play. In a Norwegian study of children's play in natural versus standardized playgrounds, Fjørtoft (2000) found that functional play such as gross-motor activities and basic skills (e.g. running, jumping, throwing, climbing, crawling, rolling, swinging and sliding) were predominant when children played in nature compared with traditional preschool play areas. Moreover, landscape structures such as steep slopes, rough cliffs and trees contributed to play activities such as climbing and sliding. According to Fjørtoft, preschoolers consider traditional playgrounds to be more boring than natural playscapes, and children develop better motor abilities when playing in nature compared with traditional playgrounds. In accordance with this notion, Kaarby (2004) studied Norwegian children's play in the natural areas of outdoor preschools and commonly observed physical activities such as climbing up steep hillsides and sliding down again, climbing up and jumping down from large rocks or small cliffs, climbing in trees, throwing javelins or cones, shooting with bows and arrows, rolling on the ground, balancing on stones, fallen trees and so on, and fencing with sticks.

The frequent use of nature as a play environment also enables kindergarten staff to offer children more challenging play environments than they would have been able to had they stayed at a standardized playground.

The forest is a natural playground where risks are present all the time: trees, streams, ponds, cliffs, etc. On the kindergarten playground, we have to follow regulations and rules for safety that do not apply in natural landscapes like the forest. Still, injuries happen inside the kindergarten house . . . when children stumble and hit their head against the table for instance . . . there are rarely any injuries in the forest.

(Norwegian preschool teacher, 27.10.09)

Both Scandinavian parents and ECEC practitioners are liberal with regard to risk during children's play and activities, and children are offered a great deal of freedom to move around and use their play environment as they like (New et al. 2005; Guldberg 2009; Sandseter 2009). According to New et al. (2005) this is because the benefits of mastering risks, experiencing various weather conditions and exploring the national landscape are widely acknowledged and encouraged in these countries. In outdoor preschools, the opportunity for children to meet physical challenges and risks are particularly likely (Sandseter 2009). These children spend most of their time in challenging natural areas, and they play in a wide range of stimulating and challenging environments.

Benefits of outdoor play

The approach to learning in Scandinavia rests on arguments that outdoor play is beneficial for children's physical, motor, psychological and social development. For instance, children's play in natural environments might benefit them because they learn about ecology and explore the environment (Bjorklund and Pellegrini 2002) and practise and enhance different motor and physical skills (Grahn et al. 1997; Fjørtoft 2000; Vigsø and Nielsen 2006) to develop muscle strength, endurance, skeletal quality, and so on (Byers and Walker 1995; Pellegrini and Smith 1998). All physical practice and training might be relevant to the developing child. Play in nature also involves the training of perceptual competencies such as depth, form, shape, size and movement perception (Fiskum 2004; Rakison 2005) as well as general spatial-orientation abilities (Bjorklund and Pellegrini 2002). Research also indicates that children show improved risk assessment and learn how to master risk situations through challenging play, especially play in wilderness areas; specifically, their subjective perception of this risk becomes more realistic (Boyesen 1997; Smith 1998; Stutz 1999; Ball 2002; Sandseter 2010, 2012). Thus, through risky play children prepare themselves for handling real risks and dangers (Adams 2001).

Outdoor activities in Scandinavian ECEC institutions are considered to be important in fulfilling the aims of developing democratic values and practice through social interactions (Aasen et al. 2009). The time spent outdoors in ECEC is primarily a time for children's free play; they can make their own choices of what and with whom to play as well as where to move. Furthermore, researchers have suggested that in outdoor play children learn how to create and recreate features in their environment so that they can actively participate in their daily lives and environments (Aasen et al. 2009). Child self-worth and independence are also strengthened by learning how to manage the environment and nature in which they live, play and explore (Nilsen 2008). Research has shown that children play more creatively in natural playgrounds (Lee 1999) and that children who play in nature are significantly more attentive and inventive than those who play on structured playgrounds (Vigsø and Nielsen 2006).

Research has also found that gender differences in play are less prominent when children play outdoors, which indicates that an outdoor environment provides the potential for more equal play and that materials in nature have fewer associations with femininity or masculinity compared with the toys inside typical ECEC settings (Sandberg and Ärlemalm-Hagsér 2011). Thus, more equal opportunities might exist outdoors for play, development and learning for both boys and girls.

One might assume that children who play outdoors in nature would develop better knowledge about nature and a higher environmental awareness. Nevertheless, this assumption has been less explored compared with how outdoor play affects the physical development, health, recreation, attentiveness, independence and creativity of children (Ejbye-Ernst 2012).

Conclusion

Scandinavian ECEC has a child-centered pedagogy that largely focuses on children's freedom and their freedom to play; furthermore, it strongly emphasizes the importance of varied and stimulating play environments. Together with a strong cultural heritage for outdoor life (friluftsliv) and an easy access to wilderness environments, ECEC has emphasized children's opportunities for outdoor play and learning in Scandinavia. Both the large number of outdoor ECEC settings and the amount of time children in ordinary ECEC settings in general spend outdoors are expressions of this emphasis. This Scandinavian ECEC approach is based on a belief that children's wellbeing, health and development are best nurtured in the outdoors. Still, there is currently a political pressure upon Scandinavian ECEC settings to introduce a stronger focus on learning, learning outcomes and school-like activities for children under school age. This has led to discussions about ECEC's content and values and how these are threatened if the focus turns from learning through play to a strong emphasis on learning outcomes. The fear is that such an emphasis could be discouraging for children's opportunity for free play and also outdoor activities. If and how the recent and ongoing policy development will change the Scandinavian ECEC is yet to be seen, but the strong cultural heritage of outdoor life in this region will most likely continue to have a great impact on pedagogical practice in Scandinavian ECEC settings.

References

Änggård, E. (2012) Att skapa platser i naturmiljöer. Om hur vardagliga praktiker i en I Ur och Skur-förskola bidrar till at ge platser identitet, *Nordic Early Childhood Education Research*, 5: 1–16.

Ärlemalm-Hagsér, E. (2008) Skogen som pedagogisk praktik ur et genusperspektiv, in A. Sandberg (ed.) *Miljöer för lek, lärande och samspel.* Lund: Studentlitteratur.

Aasen, W., Grindheim, L.T. and Waters, J. (2009) The outdoor environment as a site for children's participation, meaning-making and democratic learning: examples from Norwegian kindergartens, *Education 3–13*, 37: 5–13.

Adams, J. (2001) *Risk.* London: Routledge.

Ball, D.J. (2002) *Playgrounds: Risks, Benefits and Choices.* London: Health and Safety Executive (HSE) contract research report, Middlesex University.

Barnados and Start Strong (2012) Towards a Scandinavian childcare system for 0–12 year olds in Ireland. http://www.startstrong.ie/contents/361 (accessed 29 January 2013).

Bjorklund, D.F. and Pellegrini, A.D. (2002) *The Origins of Human Nature: Evolutionary Developmental Psychology.* Washington, DC: American Psychological Association.

Borge, A.I.H., Nordhagen, R. and Lie, K.K. (2003) Children in the environment: forest day-care centers moderen day care with historical antecedents, *The History of the Family*, 8: 605–18.

Boyesen, M. (1997) Den truende tryggheten. Unpublished doctoral thesis, The Norwegian University of Science and Technology.

Byers, J.A. and Walker, C. (1995) Refining the motor training hypothesis for the evolution of play, *The American Naturalist*, 146: 25–40.

DMSI (Danish Ministry of Social Affairs and Intergration) (2011) *Act of Pre-primary Education: LBK nr 668 af 17/06/2011.* Copenhagen: Danish Ministry of Social Affairs and Integration.

DP (Danish Parliament) (2004) *Lov om ændring af lov om social service (Pædagogiske læreplaner i dagtilbud til børn).* Copenhagen: The Danish Parliament.

Drougge, S., Kranse, C. and Friluftsfrämjandet (2007) *I ur och skur i skolan: en handledning från Friluftsfrämjandet (Outdoors in School: A Guide from Friluftsfrämjandet),* Friluftsfrämjandet.

Eilers, C. (2005) Den danske skovbørnehave – hva er det?, (The Danish outdoor preschool – what is it?) in O.B. Lysklett (ed.) *Ute hele dagen! Artikkelsamling basert på nasjonal konferanse om natur- og friluftsbarnehager* (Outdoors all Day! Conference Proceedings from the National Conference About Nature and Outdoor Preschools). Trondheim, 21–22 October 2004: Queen Maud University publication series no. 1–2005.

Ejbye-Ernst, N. (2012) Pædagogers naturformidling i naturbørnehaver (Pedagogues' communication about nature in nature preschools). PhD thesis, VIA University College.

Fiskum, T. (2004) Effekt av barnehagemiljø på motorisk og spatial kompetanse hos barn. En tverrsnittstudie av den motoriske og spatiale kompetansen hos barn i en friluftsbarnehage og barn i en tradisjonell barnehage (The effect of the preschool environment on motor and spatial competence among children. A cross-sectional study of motor and spacial competence in an outdoor preschool and a traditional preschool). Master thesis, Nord-Trøndelag University College.

Fjørtoft, I. (2000) Landscape and playscape. Learning effects from playing in a natural environment on motor development in children. PhD thesis, Norwegian School of Sport Science.

Gibson, E.J. (1988) Exploratory behavior in the development of perceiving, acting, and the acquiring of knowledge, *Annual Review of Psychology*: 1–41.

Grahn, P., Mårtensson, F., Lindblad, B., Nilsson, P. and Ekman, A. (1997) Ute på dagis. Alnarp: The University of Agriculture in Sweden.

Guldberg, H. (2009) *Reclaiming Childhood: Freedom and Play in an Age of Fear.* Abingdon: Routledge.

Heft, H. (1988) Affordances of children's environments: a functional approach to environmental description, *Children's Environments Quarterly*, 5: 29–37.

Hendry, L.B. and Kloep, M. (2002) *Lifespan Development: Resources, Challenges and Risks.* London: Thomson Learning.

Kaarby, K.M.E. (2004) Children playing in nature, in H. Schonfeld, S. O'brien and T. Walsh (eds) *Conference Proceedings*: http://www.cecde.ie/english/conference_2004.php (accessed 13 January 2014).

Kjær, B. and Olesen, J. (2005) *Informationshåndbog om pædagogiske læreplaner i dagtilbud.* Copenhagen: Danish National Board of Social Services.

Kyttä, M. (2004) The extent of children's independent mobility and the number of actualized affordances as criteria for child-friendly environments, *Journal of Environmental Psychology*, 24(2): 179–98.

Kyttä, M. (2006) Environmental child-friendliness in the light of the Bullerby Model, in C. Spencer and M. Blades (eds) *Children and Their Environments: Learning, Using and Designing Spaces.* Cambridge: Cambridge University Press.

Lee, S.-H. (1999) The cognition of playground safety and children's play – a comparison of traditional, contemporary, and naturalized playground types, in M.L. Christiansen (ed.) *Proceedings of the International Conference of Playground Safety.* Pennsylvania, PA: Penn State University: Center for Hospitality, Tourism & Recreation Research.

Little, H., Sandseter, E.B.H. and Wyver, S. (2012) Early childhood teachers' beliefs about children's risky play in Australia and Norway, *Contemporary Issues in Early Childhood*, 13: 300–16.

Lysklett, O.B. (2013) *Ute hele uka. Natur- og friluftsbarnehagen* (Outdoors All Week: The Nature and Outdoor Preschool). Oslo: Universitetsforlaget.

Lysklett, O.B., Emilsen, K. and Hagen, T.L. (2003) Hva kjennetegner natur- og friluftsbarnehager? (What characterizes nature- and outdoor preschools?), *Barnehagefolk, Pedagogisk Forum*, 4: 78–85.

Mårtensson, F. (2004) Landskapet i leken. En studie av utomhusleken på förskole-gården (The landscape of play: a study of outdoor play on the preschool play-ground). Unpublished doctoral thesis.

Moser, T. and Martinsen, M. (2010) The outdoor environment in Norwegian kinder-gartens as pedagogical space for toddlers' play, learning and development, *European Early Childhood Education Research Journal*, 18: 457–71.

New, R.S., Mardell, B. and Robinson, D. (2005) Early childhood education as risky business: going beyond what's 'safe' to discovering what is possible, *Early Childhood Research & Practice* (online), 7 (accessed 12 June 2008).

Nilsen, R.D. (2008) Children in nature: cultural ideas and social practices in Norway, in A. James and A.L. James (eds) *European Childhoods: Cultures, Politics and Childhoods in Europe*. Basingstoke: Palgrave Macmillan.

NME (2000–2001) *St.meld. nr. 39: Friluftsliv – Ein veg til høgare livskvalitet (Outdoor Life – A Road to Heightened Quality of Life)*. Oslo: Norwegian Ministry of the Environment.

NMER (Norwegian Ministry of Education and Research) (2005) *Act no. 64 of June 2005 relating to Kindergartens (the Kindergarten Act)*. Oslo: Norwegian Ministry of Education and Research.

NMER (2006/2011) *Framework Plan for the Content and Tasks of Kindergartens, issued 1. March*. Oslo: Norwegian Ministry of Education and Research.

Pellegrini, A.D. and Smith, P.K. (1998) Physical activity play: the nature and function of a neglected aspect of play, *Child Development*, 69: 577–98.

Rakison, D.H. (2005) Infant perception and cognition: an evolutionary perspective on early learning, in B.J. Ellis and D.F. Bjorklund (eds) *Origins of the Social Mind: Evolutionary Psychology and Child Development*. New York: Guilford Press.

Sandberg, A. and Ärlemalm-Hagsér, E. (2011) The Swedish National Curriculum: play and learning with fundamental values in focus, *Australasian Journal of Early Childhood*, 36: 44–50.

Sandseter, E.B.H. (2009) Affordances for risky play in preschool – the importance of features in the play environment, *Early Childhood Education Journal*, 36: 439–46.

Sandseter, E.B.H. (2010) Scaryfunny: A qualitative study of risky play among pre-school children. Unpublished doctoral thesis, Norwegian University of Science and Technology.

Sandseter, E.B.H. (2012) Restrictive safety or unsafe freedom? Norwegian ECEC practitioners' perceptions and practices concerning children's risky play, *Childcare in Practice*, 18: 83–101.

Sandseter, E.B.H., Wyver, S. and Little, H. (2012) Do theory and pedagogy have an impact on provisions for outdoor learning? A comparison of approaches in Australia and Norway, *Journal of Adventure Education and Outdoor Learning*, 12: 167–82.

SMES (Swedish Ministry of Education and Science) (1985) *Education Act (1985:1100)*. Stockholm, Swedish Ministry of Education and Science.

SMES (2010) *Curriculum for the Preschool: Lpfö 98.* Stockholm: Swedish Ministry of Education and Science, Skoleverket.

Smith, S.J. (1998) *Risk and our Pedagogical Relation to Children: On Playground and Beyond.* New York: State University of New York Press.

Stutz, E. (1999) Rethinking concepts of safety and the playground: the playground as a place in which children may learn skills for life and managing hazards, in M.L. Christiansen (ed) *Proceedings of the International Conference of Playground Safety.* Pennsylvania: Penn State University: Center for Hospitality, Tourism & Recreation Research.

Vigsø, B. and Nielsen, V. (2006) *Børn & udeliv (Children and Outdoor Life).* Esbjerg: CVU Vest Press.

9 Outdoor play in New Zealand centres: protecting, defending, extending

Alison Stephenson

Introduction

Coping with the joys – and rigours – of outdoor life was a necessity for both Māori and early European settlers. Spending time outside – boating, swimming, camping, hiking – continues to be an iconic part of the New Zealand way of life, and our bicultural heritage brings shared awareness both of the richness of our natural environment, and also our responsibility for protecting it. In the late nineteenth century, New Zealand was considered a rural paradise but now only one in seven people (population: 4,500,000) live in rural areas (Wilson 2012). The dream of each family's 'quarter acre paradise' has faded with urbanization, subdivided suburban sections and more inner-city apartment living. Increasing levels of poverty, with a growing disparity between rich and poor, have made outdoor activities and expeditions less accessible for many. Teachers are therefore increasingly aware of their responsibility for ensuring that children who attend ECE settings have access to a rich range of outdoor experiences.

Following a brief review of New Zealand research, this chapter outlines the process by which outdoor play came to be accepted as an integral part of ECE provision, identifies current pressures which threaten the quality of that provision, and describes ways in which teachers are both defending and enriching the long-established commitment to children's outdoor learning.

New Zealand research

Pairman (2012) suggests the link between physical environment and learning has been a 'blind spot' for New Zealand ECE professionals. The paucity of local research on outdoor environments and/or children's outdoor activities may be testament to that, but may also reflect the profession's justifiable satisfaction through the last decades of the twentieth century with how well we 'do' outdoor play. The few studies before the 1990s focused largely on gender, with a general consensus that boys tend to have slightly more involvement in physical and outdoor play (e.g. Halliday and McNaughton 1982; Smith 1983).

More recent research by Stephenson (2002) and Greenfield (2004, 2007) has highlighted children's enthusiasm for outdoor play. Stephenson also identified differences between indoor and outdoor environments noting the wide range of activities children participated in out of doors while Greenfield explored children's preferences for places and equipment in the playground. Other research has focused on teaching/learning outdoors (e.g. Hussain 2011; Lee 2012). Two studies perhaps reflect a growing professional unease about outdoor play provision: Greenfield (2010) investigated teachers' thoughts on what makes an optimal outdoor setting while Lockie and Wright (2002) found children in services for under 2-year-olds tended to have less free access to the outdoors.

The history of outdoor play in ECE

New Zealand has a diverse ECE sector catering for children from birth to 6 years (although typically children go to school at age 5). It includes: kindergartens, childcare (both 'for profit' and 'not for profit'), playcentres, kohanga reo (centres which focus on preserving Māori language and traditions), Pacific Island language nests, centres that represent other cultural groups, and services with a particular philosophical approach such as Steiner and Montessori. As we shall see, the kindergarten and playcentre movements were influential in providing a blueprint for outdoor play provision, but the rapid expansion in full day childcare since the 1980s has raised new issues.

Kindergartens and playcentres

While New Zealand is geographically remote, ECE here has been influenced by European thinkers. Within the kindergarten movement – the main form of ECE until the late twentieth century – Froebel was particularly influential. A number of early teachers and training directors were Froebel trained (Simpson 1970) which ensured his commitment to children engaging with nature was embedded in the philosophical approach. Later, the open-air nursery established by the McMillan sisters in London in the early twentieth century inspired New Zealand teachers who read about it or visited (May 1997). The contribution of the kindergarten movement was that it provided a high-quality standard for the design and provision of playgrounds.

The first kindergartens were set up at the end of the nineteenth century with a focus on 'rescuing' the children of the poor. They had no outdoor areas (May 1997) but in fine weather the children might be taken to the park 'or by special invitation to private gardens' (Hughes 1989: 11); however, when the Créche and

Kindergarten Association was formed in 1911, the ideal of 'light airy buildings with pretty gardens' (Downer 1964: 32) was established, although in reality many kindergartens still opened in hired halls with limited outdoor areas while funds were raised (Simpson 1970). The first purpose-built kindergarten only opened in 1914 (Hughes 1989: 11). Gradually provision of outdoor play areas became the norm. A 1916 kindergarten had an outdoor area containing 'about 65 tiny flower-beds, so that each child could be taught elementary gardening, and be the proud owner of his or her individual plot' (Marshall 1983: 17). A 1926 kindergarten had 'a verandah, 60 feet by 10 feet, along the entire front, glazed at the ends. It was built on almost half an acre of land adjoining playing fields and was surrounded by lawns, trees, paths and trolley tracks' (Hughes 1989: 16). One of the earliest so-called 'open air kindergartens' – a purpose-built kindergarten with wide doors opening to the outdoors – opened in 1936 (Sewell and Bethell 2009). By 1953 the government was requiring kindergartens to open in their own buildings (Simpson 1970), and the 1952 guidelines for playgrounds were: 'A site of a quarter of an acre with a sufficient proportion of flat or nearly flat land was the ideal, with maximum sun and shelter from the wind. All the trees, irregularities of the ground and any special features were to be kept. Part of the area was to be paved, the rest laid out in a garden with a place for digging' (Hughes 1989: 15).

The provisioning for outdoor activity was also changing. A teacher recalling kindergarten in the 1920s remembered 'carpentry, waterplay, sand, swings, tricycles and balls' (Middleton and May 1997: 31) suggesting outdoor activities were well established. By the 1950s the playground was likely to include a sandpit, jungle gym, swings and large wooden car crates and reels. Other equipment, such as a slide, carts, ladders and planks, carpentry table and tools, were kept in a shed. Tricycles were not then considered suitable equipment (Eggleston 2006).

The kindergarten movement was significant because it established a benchmark of the ECE playground as a spacious, well-provisioned area with natural features. However, as Pairman (2012) notes, kindergartens were traditionally for 3- to 5-year-olds attending on a sessional basis, and not designed for younger children, for mixed age groups or for full day attendance.

The first playcentre, founded by a group of mothers in 1941, was intended to provide mutual support while husbands were away at war. As the movement grew, the focus expanded to include education for parents as well as for children. Each centre was run as a parent cooperative, with children attending up to three sessions a week, and parents rostered as supervisors. The contribution of the early playcentre movement was that it shifted the ground on children's access to the outdoors, and on the value placed on learning in that environment.

Susan Isaacs had toured New Zealand in 1937 and her lectures on progressive education – on equality through education, and on developing the personality of each child – inspired both teachers and policy makers. The playcentre movement readily adopted these ideals, underpinned by an image of the child as an emerging individual with physical, intellectual and moral capacities to be nurtured. A free play approach was integral (May 1997) – an approach less readily accepted within kindergartens.

Allowing children freedom to choose was aligned with free access to the outdoors: 'We like to think of the New Zealand play centre movement as an out-door movement and encourage as much work out of doors' (Somerset 1964: 10). The 'work' included sandplay, waterplay, science and nature, junk play, messy play, physical play and carpentry; they were among the 16 stipulated areas of play. The value of learning through outdoor experiences was reiterated in publications and training. The ideal of 'free flow' was introduced with children able to move freely between inside and outside for most of the session – 'We try to arrange the space so that both indoors and outdoors can be used at will on a fine day' (Somerset 1964: 10). This was made easier by the higher adult:child ratio required in playcentres.

This was in contrast to the kindergarten sessions of the 1940s that tended to be tightly structured with children, divided into groups, being rotated through prescribed activities: 'Somehow, during the morning each group had to have music, story or talk, wash time, a rest, handwork, outdoor play, etc.' (Eva Millen, quoted in Eggleston 2006: 22). By the mid-century policy makers were promoting the 'learning through play' approach (May 2009) and kindergarten teachers were encouraged to relax their programmes. Initial brief periods of free activity (May 1997) extended in the 1950s to children being allowed to choose between indoor and outdoor activities for the first hour, and messier play activities such as finger and foot painting were tried (Eggleston 2006). Some teachers took a more wholehearted approach:

> We didn't have a timetable, we just let them free, let them do what they wanted to. We let the big boys go outside. You could see them sitting on the mat bored to tears, bored absolutely bored. They played outside nearly all the morning, and the difference in them! We even let them go to the toilet when they wanted to.
>
> (Joyce Barnes, quoted in May 2009: 20)

Through the 1950s, 'free flow' gradually became the accepted norm, and by 1966, both kindergartens and playcentres were said to offer 'long periods of indoor and outdoor play with a minimum of routine period' with the advisory comment that outdoor time depending on the weather being 'favourable' (Gallagher 1966). Then, as now, 'favourable' weather is typically considered to be when it is not raining heavily or very cold.

The emergence of full day education and care centres

Childcare centres had existed since the late 19th century to provide unregu-lated care for children of working women. There are only occasional glimpses of how children's outdoor play may have been provided for. A photograph of the crèche opened by the Sisters of Compassion in 1903 shows children in wicker prams 'getting fresh air and sunshine outside' (Tennant 2012). A popular Auckland department store opened a roof-top playground in 1922 for the children of shoppers. A community childcare centre, opened in 1937 on the roof top of the new railway station, included 'a large playroom opening on to a play area with a sandpit' (May 1997: 102–3). It wasn't until 1960 that the first child-care centre regulations were introduced, and only in 1989 were early childhood education and care integrated, and a single regulatory framework established to cover all services.

Since the 1980s, the growth of the childcare sector has changed the face of ECE provision in New Zealand. Large commercial providers, which appeared in the late 1970s, flourished with increasing government investment in ECE, and have introduced new pressures. Now childcare – both for profit and not for profit – is the predominant service type, and the proportion of for-profit services has increased. More children are now enrolled in education and care centres (as childcare is increasingly called) than in all other services combined. The number of children regularly attending for full days has spiralled, and the enrolment of children from birth to 2 years has also jumped dramatically (ECE Task Force 2010). These changes in enrolment patterns raise important questions:

- Is the quality of outdoor play provision, established in sessional kindergartens and playcentres, appropriate for children attending full day centres?
- Do current legislative requirements adequately protect those high standards of provision that evolved through the last century?

The remainder of this chapter describes some ways in which current legislative requirements reflect a diminished commitment to outdoor play, and then offers examples of how teachers are both defending and extending those earlier visions of quality.

Current regulations: pressure or protection?

Te Whāriki

The national curriculum, Te Whāriki, became a requirement for services in 1998. The philosophical approach in Te Whāriki is that each centre will weave its own version of the curriculum, 'to meet the needs of its children, their families, the specific setting, and the local community' (Ministry of Education 1996: 27). Reflecting this approach there are few requirements linked to particular aspects of the environment. No goal specifically refers to the outdoor environment, and only a few learning outcomes indicate the need to go outdoors: for example, two of the learning outcomes for the goal 'Children experience an environment where they develop working theories for making sense of the natural, social, physical, and material worlds' (Ministry of Education 1996: 90) are:

- Children develop a relationship with the natural environment and a knowledge of their own place in the environment
- Children develop respect and a developing sense of responsibility for the well-being of both the living and the non-living environment
                                          (Ministry of Education 1996: 90)

The most specific requirements in relation to the outdoors are in the 'Adults' Responsibilities in Management, Organisation, and Practice':

- 'Daily routines should . . . allow for frequent outdoor experiences' (Ministry of Education 1996: 47);
- 'Both indoor and outdoor environments, including the neighbourhood, should be used as learning resources' (Ministry of Education 1996: 83).

The 2008 regulations

The regulations provide more explicit detail. The Licensing Criteria for Early Childhood Education and Care Centres,[1] which came into effect in 2008, state the requirements for services to meet the standards of the 2008 regulations.[2] While the Criteria largely protect young children's outdoor activities there are some details that potentially diminish the earlier visions of quality. The impact of the Licensing Criteria are considered in relation to:

- children's access to the outdoors;
- the minimum requirements for the outdoor area (including space requirements and provision of quiet places);
- the quality of outdoor experiences (including acknowledging our bicultural heritage, contact with nature and risk-taking).

These issues are therefore discussed below.

Children's access to the outdoors

While children's access to an outdoor playspace is – for most – protected in legislation, there are signs the ground is shifting. First, until 1991, the vision

---

[1]Electronic copies of the Licensing criteria for centre-based services are available at http://www.lead.ece.govt.nz
[2]The current regulations are available online at http://www.legislation.govt.nz/regulation/public/2008/0204/latest/DLM1412501.html

of 'an easy flow of play between the indoor and outdoor spaces at all times' (Ministry of Education 1990: 3) was upheld in the official document, the DOPS.[3] Legislative changes since then have diminished that freedom of access in response to lobbying from the education and care sector. For example, the 1991 changes made it possible for one centre to be licensed where children needed to be accompanied by an adult across a carpark and driveway to reach a fenced playground. The same changes allowed the outdoor playspace to be a balcony in a high-rise building, reflecting some earlier childcare provision, but at odds with the playground standards established in kindergartens and play-centres. Now the 2008 Licensing Criteria require that: 'The design and layout of the premises support effective adult supervision so that children's access to the licensed space (indoor and outdoor) is not unnecessarily limited' (PF2) (Premises and facilities criterion 2) and that the 'Outdoor activity space is connected to the indoor activity space and can be easily and safely accessed by children' (PF 13). While the associated 'Rationale/Intent' states that 'outdoor play is an important feature of the education and care of young children', the Criteria wording is nevertheless a significant shift from the earlier commitment to 'an easy flow . . . at all times'. It seems that official commitment to ensuring young children's sustained access to the outdoors is diminishing. A recent recommendation from the Education Review Office (2009: 8) that some infant and toddler centres need 'to review both the time available to children for outdoor play, and its accessibility' reiterates this concern.

Second, since 1991 children attending crèche facilities in settings such as gyms and swimming pools are unlikely to have any access to the outdoors. The 2008 regulations retain the 1991 dispensation for providing outdoor spaces in such centres if children attend for no more than two hours a day.

Finally, for some children, Resource Consent conditions limit their outdoor access. Noise is a frequent concern for potential neighbours, and Consent conditions can include limiting the hours in which children can access the outdoors, prohibiting music or use of a stereo out of doors and/or limiting the number of children outside at any time. A news report underlines the impact these may have:

> The co-owner . . . says they have spent a lot of money to reduce noise. She says a consultant told her a fence wouldn't help and council rules won't allow a higher one. She says the childcare centre works hard to minimise noise . . . but it's impossible to tell a child to be quiet when they're happy and excited. 'We try to say use a quiet voice'. Among measures already taken is spending $500 to lay carpet outside on the deck.
>
> (Willis 2012, (c) Fairfax New Zealand News)

---

[3] 'The DOPS' is the common abbreviation for the *Early Childhood Education Charter Guidelines: A Statement of Desirable Objectives and Practices* (Ministry of Education 1990). Implementing the DOPS was mandatory for all chartered services.

The number and severity of such imposed conditions are taken into account in deciding if a licence will be granted.

Minimum requirements

Minimum space requirements

The 2008 Regulations retain the previous minimum requirement of 5 square metres of outdoor space per child (and 2.5 square metres indoors). This minimum has had little impact on kindergartens and playcentres, which typically continue to provide larger areas, but has been used to define playground size in some other centres. International comparisons emphasize how minimal the outdoor requirement is. Pairman (2012: 25) reports Australian recommendations range from 7 to 25 square metres per child, and that the OECD average requirement is '8.9 m^2 for younger children, and 7 m^2 for older children'. Age does not influence New Zealand requirements.

The widespread practice of not allowing children outside in inclement weather makes the minimal space requirement of greater concern, although many centres do allow children some semi-outdoor access in bad weather by using roll-down plastic walls to weatherproof a porch area. This can provide a cooler/calmer/quieter environment and/or a setting for messy play or physical activities.

Other requirements

The legislation contains few other specific requirements. The playground needs to be 'safe, well-drained, and suitably surfaced for a variety of activities' (PF13) and the design and layout of the premises need to:

- support the provision of different types of indoor and outdoor experiences; and
- include quiet spaces, areas for physically active play, and space for a range of individual and group learning experiences appropriate to the number, ages, and abilities of children attending. (PF1)

A further criterion, applying only to services with children under 2 years, is that there need to be safe spaces for non-walking children where they are 'protected from more mobile children' (PF14).

Providing protected spaces for younger children and/or quiet retreat spaces outdoors can be challenging for centres with only minimal outdoor space. It can be particularly challenging for the many centres operating from a converted house, where turning the space around a dwelling into an easily supervised area can lead to sections being fenced off and/or having two different play areas which are used at different times. The unchallenged requirement that a teacher must be outside whenever a child/children are outside can lead to the scheduling of set outdoor periods in order to alleviate pressure on staff rosters, and can exacerbate the difficulty of providing quiet/protected spaces.

Reviewing current legislation on children's outdoor access and minimum space requirements therefore indicates areas for concern, where long-established standards are potentially being eroded, particularly within the education and care sector. The following section will describe some ways in which teachers are defending and extending those earlier visions of young children's free flow access to an enriching outdoor play environment.

The quality of outdoor experiences

As Greenfield's (2010) research showed, New Zealand teachers value a range of qualities in outdoor playspaces that extend far beyond the legislated requirements. Here the focus is on three aspects that are currently influencing – and extending – discussion about outdoor play provision. Acknowledging our bicultural heritage is particular to New Zealand, while a commitment to engaging children with the natural world, and to offering experiences of risk and challenge reflect wider international trends.

Acknowledging our bicultural heritage

A commitment to biculturalism is fundamental to *Te Whāriki*, reflecting the Treaty of Waitangi, signed between the Crown and the Māori people in 1840, and which continues to underpin our constitutional foundations. In some centres a commitment to biculturalism is relatively superficial, but in others teachers are passionate about this commitment.

Some incorporate traditional Māori patterns and designs as decorative features in fencing, play structures and/or surfacing, or have a mural of native flora and fauna. Others use natural materials within their outdoor setting – for example, a fence of driftwood, punga (fern) trunks, or flax stalks; shells set into paving, native plants in a wilderness area. Some teachers use Māori names for plants and animals; others acknowledge deeper Māori values and traditions, such as respect for the natural world. Teachers at a kindergarten with a long-standing commitment to biculturalism and sustainability, wrote in their application to be a Centre of Innovation:

> The culture of Otaki Kindergarten fosters responsibility for Papatu-anuku [the land, a mother earth figure] and Ranginui [the sky father]: Te Ao Maori [the Maori world]. Environmental education is an essential part of the curriculum – simply because we are all a part of the earth. We aspire to become kaitiaki, mindful caretakers of our patch of the world. By adhering to this philosophy, the teachers encourage

tamariki [children] to be active participants, contributing to their part of the world.

(Ministry of Education 2009)

Unfortunately funding was withdrawn, and the Centre of Innovation process ended before the research was completed.

Contact with nature

There is no reference to providing contact with nature in the Licensing Criteria, but the 'Guidance examples' which show how services might meet the requirements state: 'Outdoor space should enable children to experience natural settings (e.g. wind, sky, sun, rain)' – but interestingly no references to soil, plants or animals. Making contact with the natural world – with grass, trees, animals – is challenging for centres with playgrounds on balconies. But in any centre, replacing grass and soil with artificial surfacing can seem practical, both because the area can be used immediately after rain, and because children are less likely to get dirty. This trend was highlighted when a concern about the lack of grass areas, gardens and natural resources in some infant and toddler services was raised (Education Review Office 2009).

Although relatively barren playgrounds dominated by manufactured structures and artificial surfaces do exist, there are many centres where teachers are passionate about enhancing children's contact with nature, introducing broader notions of sustainability and taking children regularly beyond the immediate playground into areas of bush, farmland or reserve. Even inner-city centres often have small plots for growing vegetables and may keep animals such as chickens, rabbits or frogs. The outdoor area of one suburban childcare centre includes vegetable gardens, a butterfly garden and fruit trees. In a kindergarten with a philosophical commitment to sustainability a focus on growing fruit and vegetables has expanded into food preparation. Centres in rural areas often have more expansive settings. For example, a centre with a strong focus on the natural world includes wild areas, driftwood logs for climbing, native plantings, fruit trees and organic gardens (Geelen 2010). In another centre with expansive grounds, children help care for miniature horses, chickens, guinea pigs, turtles, fish and frogs, as well as learning about composting and worm farming (Goodison and Kimber 2010).

Some centres have joined the New Zealand-based Enviroschools programme which introduces students – in centres and schools – to sustainable living as they work towards a series of awards. In one playcentre children and adults conducted a waste audit by categorizing the contents of two days of the rubbish, and discovered about a quarter of their rubbish could have been composted or recycled. They now recycle metal, glass and plastic, have a thriving wormery living on kitchen and lunchbox scraps and plan to create a compost system (The Enviroschools Foundation 2013).

As teachers read about – and visit – forest kindergartens in Europe, enthusiasm for that movement is growing; however, implementing those ideas has not been easy. One teacher, enthused by a visit to Denmark in 2005, eventually concluded 'safety-obsessed New Zealand' might not be ready for the approach. The official response was that the Regulations 'do not restrict children playing in public places, going outside in all weather or taking risks, but that preschools must ensure the safety and well-being of children. They must also have plumbing and electricity, and provide 2.5 m^2 of indoor space for each child' (Harward 2009 (c) Fairfax New Zealand News).

Despite the documentation required for taking children on excursions, many teachers are introducing regular trips, undertaken in all weathers, to natural areas – a local reserve, an area of native forest, the surrounding rural area, or to visiting a planting of ancient trees (Brownlee and Daly 2009). Typically the emphasis is on the natural world, encouraging children to take the lead and providing equipment such as magnifying glasses and binoculars. A few centres in rural areas incorporate large natural areas and so can avoid the required documentation for excursions.

Challenge and risk

A concern with safety remains to the fore in legislation. While, as noted above, there is a perception that New Zealand is currently 'safety obsessed', this 'official' concern with safety is not new: 'In the 1950s, parents and the Health Department . . . distrusted water play. There were "germs" in water; water brought about bronchitis and drowning, so ban water play. Cut out sandpits, use sand trays. Sandpits are where cats "toilet". . . . "Merciful heavens! That's not a saw, a chisel, hammer that child has, is it?" Banish it' (Lex Grey, cited in Stover 2003: 10). Over time, compliance requirements for teachers/owners have increased. The onus for showing that playground equipment and facilities meet specified safety standards, and/or are installed correctly now rests with the service provider (PF5). Centres also need to have a hazard identification and management system showing premises and equipment are maintained regularly. Specified outdoor hazards include: 'vandalism, dangerous objects, and foreign materials (e.g. broken glass, animal droppings); equipment faults; poisonous plants; and bodies of water'. Finally, centres need to ensure gates and fences effectively contain children (PF13).

While sporadic media discussions suggest an overemphasis on safety is leading to a generation of 'cotton-wool kids' the regulations make no mention of providing children with risk-taking opportunities. New Zealand research confirms international findings that many children relish the opportunity to extend themselves physically. Greenfield (2007) found children (aged 2 to 5 years) preferred spaces that allowed them the chance to be active, practise new skills and take risks. Their preference was for the large movable equipment, and particularly for the horizontal ladders (the 'monkey bars') which provided them with the potential to set themselves increasingly demanding challenges.

Stephenson (2003: 36) identified the elements that made an experience seem 'risky' to a 4-year-old were: 'attempting something never done before; feeling on the borderline of "out of control" often because of height or speed, and overcoming fear', and saw a similar focus among very young children.

Working with successive cohorts of ECE teacher trainees I have been heartened that their own childhood memories almost always lead them to a belief that children need to have opportunities to experience challenge and feelings of risk. An unexpected, recent trend is an interest in promoting rough and tumble play. Some students have set up and facilitated sessions – with teachers' and parents' permission – where children wrestle with peers. Given international research on the potential value of rough and tumble play (Tannock 2008), this is a development to watch with interest.

Maintaining the focus

As this chapter has shown, legislative changes, often driven by commercial pressures, are leading to some playgrounds being designed to meet minimum standards rather than providing children with that sheltered, sunny spacious play area envisaged in the kindergarten standards. Similarly, legislative changes have diminished children's right to the free flow of access between inside and outside, established first in early playcentre practices. Despite this many New Zealand teachers are demonstrating their commitment to defending and extending those earlier standards, and to protecting their vision of quality outdoor play provision.

References

Brownlee, P. and Daly, C. (2009) Open spaces, *The Space for Anything about Early Childhood*, 17: 7–8.

Downer, H. (1964) *Seventy-five Years of Free Kindergartens in New Zealand*. Wellington: NZ Free Kindergarten Union.

ECE Task Force (2010) *Overview of the NZ Early Childhood Education System*. http://www.taskforce.ece.govt.nz/wp-content/uploads/2010/11/1-Overview-of-the-NZ-Early-Childhood-Education-System.pdf (accessed 31 March 2013).

Education Review Office (2009) *The Quality of Education and Care in Infant and Toddler Centres*. Wellington: Education Review Office.

Eggleston, C. (2006) *Kindergarten: A Great Place to Start*. Christchurch, NZ: Carol Eggleston.

Gallagher (1966) Education, preschool, in A.H. McLintock (ed.) *Te Ara: The Encyclopaedia of New Zealand*. http://www.TeAra.govt.nz/en/1966/education-preschool (accessed 2 March 2013).

Geelen, A. (2010) Little Earth Montessori, *The Space for Anything about Early Childhood*, 21: 12.

Goodison, M. and Kimber, A. (2010) Matapihi Kindergarten, *The Space for Anything about Early Childhood*, 19: 12–13.

Greenfield, C. (2004) 'Can run, play on bikes, jump the zoom slide, and play on swings': exploring the value of outdoor play, *Australian Journal of Early Childhood*, 29(2): 1–5.

Greenfield, C. (2007) What is it about the monkey bars? *Early Childhood Folio*, 11: 31–5.

Greenfield, C. (2010) Characteristics of optimal early childhood centre outdoor environments: spaces and places in which children and adults want to be, *New Zealand Research in Early Childhood*, 15: 46–60.

Halliday, J. and McNaughton, S. (1982) Sex differences in play at kindergarten, *New Zealand Journal of Educational Studies*, 17(2): 161–72.

Harward E. (2009) A really wild way to grow kids. http://www.stuff.co.nz/national/education/2929419/A-really-wild-way-to-grow-kids (c) Fairfax New Zealand News (accessed 7 April 2013).

Hughes, B. (1989) *Flags and Building Blocks, Formality and Fun: One Hundred Years of Free Kindergarten in New Zealand.* Wellington: NZ Free Kindergarten Union.

Hussain, H. (2011) Exploring games of chase in the early childhood curriculum, *Early Childhood Folio*, 15: 22–6.

Lee, S. (2012) Toddlers as mathematicians, *Australasian Journal of Early Childhood*, 37(1): 30–7.

Lockie, C. and Wright, J. (2002) The golden kiwi childhood: is it a lottery? *New Zealand Research in Early childhood Education*, 5: 157–67.

Marshall, B. (1983) *A History of the Auckland Kindergarten Association.* Auckland: Auckland Kindergarten Association.

May, H. (1997) *The Discovery of Early Childhood.* Auckland: Auckland University Press/Bridget Williams Books.

May, H. (2009) *Politics in the Playground: The World of Early Childhood in New Zealand.* Dunedin: Otago University.

Middleton, S. and May, H. (1997) *Teachers Talk Teaching 1915–1995.* Palmerston North: Dunmore.

Ministry of Education (1990) *Early Childhood Education Charter Guidelines: Statement of Desirable Objectives and Practices.* Wellington: Ministry of Education.

Ministry of Education (1996) *Te Whāriki: Early Childhood Curriculum.* Wellington: Learning Media.

Ministry of Education (2009) Otaki kindergarten. http://www.educate.ece.govt.nz/EducateHome/Programmes/CentresOfInnovation/RoundFour/OtakiKindergarten.aspx (accessed 13 March 2013).

Pairman, A. (2012) The relationship between the physical environment and learning: a blind spot in New Zealand early childhood education discourse, *New Zealand Annual Review of Education*, 21: 21–45.

Sewell, A. and Bethell, K. (2009) Building interests: a 1940s story of curriculum innovation and contemporary connections, *New Zealand Journal of Teachers' Work*, 6(2): 93–110.

Simpson, M. (1970) *The Free Kindergarten Movement in New Zealand*. New Zealand: The New Zealand Free Kindergarten Union.

Smith, A.B. (1983) Sex differences in activities in early childhood centres, *New Zealand Journal of Psychology*, 12: 74–81.

Somerset, G. (1964) *Play and How to Provide for it*. Wellington: Wellington Play Centres Association.

Stephenson, A. (2002) Opening up the outdoors: exploring the relationship between the indoor and outdoor environments of a centre, *European Early Childhood Education Research Journal*, 10(1): 29–38.

Stephenson, A. (2003) Physical risk-taking: dangerous or endangered? *Early Years*, 23(1): 35–43.

Stover, S. (2003) *Good Clean Fun: New Zealand's Playcentre Movement*. Auckland: NZ Playcentre Federation.

Tannock, M.T. (2008) Rough and tumble play: an investigation of the perceptions of educators and young children, *Early Childhood Education Journal*, 35: 357–61.

Tennant, M. (2012) Voluntary welfare organisations: 19th century charity, *Te Ara: The Encyclopaedia of New Zealand*. http://www.TeAra.govt.nz/en/photograph/29045/sisters-of-compassion (accessed 5 April 2013).

The Enviroschools Foundation (2013) Watching our waste. http://www.enviroschools.org.nz/in_your_region/wellington/early-years/watching-our-waste (accessed 7 April 2013).

Willis, L. (2012) Couple seeks noise fence. http://www.stuff.co.nz/auckland/local-news/north-shore-times/7144077/Couple-seeks-noise-fence (c) Fairfax New Zealand News (accessed 12 April 2013).

Wilson, J. (2012) Society: where New Zealanders live, *Te Ara: The Encyclopaedia of New Zealand*. http://www.TeAra.govt.nz/en/society/page-2 (accessed 28 February 2013).

10 Outdoor play in Australia

Helen Little and Shirley Wyver

Introduction

Australia is known for its vast open spaces and beaches. The iconic image of the 'bronzed Aussie' is in contrast to the reality of a population who prefer to keep children indoors, behind fences or at least very close to home and have in recent decades become increasingly risk averse (Wyver et al. 2010). In this chapter, we start with a very brief overview of some aspects of the history of Australia to examine dramatic cultural changes leading to the majority population lifestyle being poorly connected to the natural environment. We examine contradictions between the iconic image and reality of Australian life and consider how a mismatch between perception and reality of freedom in Australia may have contributed to the over-regulation of outdoor play in a range of areas, including early childhood services. The second part of this chapter examines Australia's current early childhood arrangements in the context of the three-tiered government structure that has been in place since federation. While we cover the entire early childhood period and the associated education/care sectors in this chapter, our strongest focus is on the preschool period (3–5 years). This is mainly driven by availability of research.

Rapid urbanization

Before white settlement, just over 200 years ago, Australian culture was inextricably linked with the land (Flannery 1994). Although some Indigenous Australians retain a traditional lifestyle, rapid changes have occurred since white settlement. At 23 million, the Australian population is low relative to most countries, but it is one of the most rapidly growing populations with cultural practices that are in direct conflict with the natural environment, such as designing housing areas which accumulate fire fuel and are therefore vulnerable in hot, dry summer months (Flannery 1994). Australia has approximately three people per square kilometre of land (ABS 2010), yet 88.6 per cent of Australians live in a small number of urban areas (Trading Economics 2013).

As will be discussed in detail, outdoor areas in childcare centres and schools are often small, overcrowded and lack opportunities for risky play.

National image

Many argue that the dominant contemporary image of Australians emerged after the Second World War. Artist Brendan Lee (2011) suggests 'Australian national identity was built upon hard masculine foundations, using the harsh nature of the bush to exemplify these character traits' and this is the image popularized overseas through characters and personalities such as Crocodile Dundee and Steve Irwin. Children give priority to the natural elements such as animals and landscape when identifying uniquely Australian characteristics (Howard and Gill 2001), yet recent analyses indicate Australian children are less physically active than they would like to be, their screen-time is excessive and an increase in environments that restrict free movement have contributed to escalating levels of obesity (Dollman et al. 2005).

In the 1980s–90s, a new image of the aspirational class replaced previous images of working-class Australians. According to Hosking the new image of aspirational Australians 'unencumbered by traditional political allegiance, practical, ambitious, rationally self-interested, hard-working and unsentimentally materialistic' (2011: 1) has persisted despite the lack of an evidentiary basis. Importantly, this image has been a conduit for neo-liberalist reforms. For prior-to-school care, neo-liberalist reforms have been apparent in the shift from community-based to market-based care including a publicly listed childcare corporation (ABC Learning) (Brennan 2007).

Sectors, systems and qualifications

ECE in Australia for children aged 3–7 years encompasses two main education sectors: prior-to-school including long day care (LDC – catering for children from birth to 6 years), preschool (for children 3 to 5 years; also referred to as kindergarten in some states), and school (catering for children from 5 years of age). Each sector has different requirements for staff qualifications and regulations regarding outdoor provision.

The prior-to-school sector is in transition as a consequence of significant government reforms introduced from 2009. The change of the Australian Government in 2007 heralded a renewed focus on ECE with moves towards a national approach to quality and service provision and a commitment to universal access to ECE for all Australian children in the year prior to commencing full-time schooling (Waniganayake et al. 2012). Under the National Quality Framework, these reforms focus on three main initiatives: the National Quality Standards and the introduction of a national early years learning framework;

National Law and Regulations; and a quality rating system (Productivity Commission 2011). ECE provision is further complicated by the three tiers of government (federal, state/territory, local) each having involvement in service provision as well as the historical divisions between 'education' and 'care'. In line with the Australian government reforms discussed above, responsibility for prior-to-school and school education now falls under the jurisdiction of the education portfolio in most states/territories (except Western Australia).

Responsibility for school education lies mainly with the state/territory governments and consequently there is great variation, for example, in relation to the minimum school starting age which ranges from 4.5–5 years. To address some of the variations, changes have occurred in the school education sector with the move from individual states/territories having responsibility for curriculum to the development of a national curriculum. The reasons and debates surrounding this move are complex but the two most cited reasons are to allow for greater ease of movement of students between states and to raise educational standards in response to Australian students' poorer than anticipated performance on international tests in literacy, numeracy and science (Drabsch 2013).

To contextualize the discussion of outdoor play provision in the later sections of this chapter, Table 10.1 provides an overview of teacher qualifications, curriculum, and regulatory and accreditation requirements for each sector, highlighting the ECE reforms and the complexity of issues relating to the different sectors.

Regulatory environment

In this section, we examine the regulatory environment and other requirements in prior-to-school settings and schools that influence outdoor play provision. In particular, we focus on factors that potentially present barriers to outdoor play and pedagogy.

Outdoor play provision in prior-to-school settings is influenced by three main documents: National Regulations, National Quality Standard (NQS), and the Early Years Learning Framework (EYLF). The EYLF provides guidance for early childhood educators' pedagogy and curriculum decision-making (Australian Government Department of Education, Employment and Workplace Relations [DEEWR] 2009). In relation to outdoor learning environments it has the following to say:

> Outdoor learning spaces are a feature of Australian learning environments. They offer a vast array of possibilities not available indoors. Play spaces in natural environments include plants, trees, edible gardens, sand, rocks, mud, water and other elements from nature. These spaces invite open-ended interactions, spontaneity, risk-taking, exploration, discovery and connection with nature.
>
> (DEEWR 2009: 15–16)

Table 10.1 Overview of qualifications, curriculum and regulatory requirements for prior-to-school and school sectors

	Prior-to-school				School
	Long day care		Preschool/kindergarten		
	Pre-2011/2012	Current	Pre-2011/2012	Current	
Teacher qualifications	Varied by jurisdiction:[2] 3 or 4 year university degree Diploma[3]	3 or 4 year university degree[4] Diploma	3 or 4 year university degree	4 year university degree	4 year university degree
Licensing and regulation	Mandatory licensing[2] – conditions varied across states/territories Regulation of staff, program and premises[2] – varied across states/territories Visits and spot checks	National Law and Regulations[1] – provider and service approval; supervisor certificates; minimum operational requirements in relation to the 7 quality areas of the NQS; process for rating and assessment of services[2] against NQS including rating levels	Varied by jurisdiction – some required licensing others required registration only	National Law and Regulations[1] – provider and service approval; supervisor certificates; minimum operational requirements in relation to the 7 quality areas of the NQS; process for rating and assessment of services[2] against NQS including rating levels	Relevant Education Acts in each state/territory[2]

Quality accreditation	NCAC quality accreditation – 10 quality areas (incorporating 35 principles) including learning and development relationships with children and families, staffing and premises[1] Validation visits and surveys	NQS administered by ACECQA – 7 quality areas (educational program and practice; health and safety; physical environment; staffing; relationships with children; family and community partnerships; leadership and management) with 17 accompanying standards[1] NQF rating system – assessor visits[2]	None but optional registration with NCAC[1]	NQS administered by ACECQA – 7 quality areas (educational program and practice; health and safety; physical environment; staffing; relationships with children; family and community partnerships; leadership and management) with 17 accompanying standards[1] NQF rating system – assessor visits[2]	ACARA – responsible for collecting, managing, analysing, evaluating and reporting statistical and related information about educational outcomes. Development of national key performance measures for reporting the performance of Australian schooling[1] AITSL – Australian Professional Standards for Teachers and teacher certification[1]

(Continued)

Table 10.1 Overview of qualifications, curriculum and regulatory requirements for prior-to-school and school sectors (Continued)

	Prior-to-school				School
	Long day care		Preschool/kindergarten		
	Pre-2011/2012	Current	Pre-2011/2012	Current	
Curriculum	Varied by jurisdiction – not all states/territories had a curriculum framework Voluntary implementation in some states	Early Years Learning Framework (EYLF) or other approved learning framework[1]	Varied by jurisdiction – not all states/territories had a curriculum framework Voluntary implementation in some states	Early Years Learning Framework (EYLF)[1] or other approved learning framework[1] e.g. Australian Capital Territory: Every Chance to Learn – Curriculum framework for ACT schools preschool to Year 10	State/Territory developed curriculum[2] (e.g. NSW Board of Studies curriculum) Australian Curriculum[1] (ACARA) – English, mathematics, science and history for Foundation to Year 10 Curriculum introduced. Geography, languages, the arts, health and physical education, technologies, economics and business and civics and citizenship are under development[5]. Education authorities in each state/territory have responsibility for implementation[2] of the Australian Curriculum and for supporting schools and teachers

Notes: 1 – Australian Government responsibility; 2 – State/Territory authority/department responsibility; 3 – one year vocational qualification; 4 – four year university degree required for teachers delivering preschool program in LDC; 5 – The Australian curriculum is being gradually phased in from 2013. ACARA – Australian Curriculum, Assessment and Reporting Authority; ACECQA – Australian Children's Education and Care Quality Authority; AITSL – Australian Institute for Teaching and School Leadership; NCAC – National Childcare Accreditation Council; NQF – National Quality Framework; NQS – National Quality Standards.

Sources: ACECQA 2011a; Productivity Commission 2011; Waniganayake et al. 2012.

The EYLF also emphasizes the educators' role in planning and implementing learning through play and intentional teaching that actively promotes children's learning through meaningful and challenging experiences, and creating learning environments that respond flexibly to children's interests and abilities (DEEWR 2009); however, these pedagogical aims need to be met in conjunction with the requirements of the National Regulations and NQS within each of the Quality Areas. Previous studies (Fenech et al. 2006; Bown and Sumsion 2007) examining the impact of the regulatory environment have found that teachers experience tension in providing learning environments for children that reflect their pedagogical aims and balancing this against their accountability requirements. The teachers in these studies felt that their focus was more on compliance with regulatory requirements which limited their capacity to use their pedagogic knowledge to inform their practice. While these studies were conducted at a time when the previous regulations were in force, it remains to be seen whether the current reforms have improved the situation.

To understand the links between the various regulatory requirements and the discussion of their potential influence on outdoor play provision, Table 10.2 provides an overview of the National Regulations and NQS quality areas and accompanying standards. While all the quality areas and standards ultimately influence the learning opportunities provided for children, only those that have specific relevance to outdoor play provision have been included.

While the EYLF promotes the importance of children engaging in challenging experiences that involve risk-taking, this is mediated by teachers' accountability under the National Regulations and NQS. Under the National Law, centres 'must take reasonable care to protect children from foreseeable risk of harm, injury or infection' (ACECQA 2011b: 50). In terms of Quality Area 2, this means 'monitoring and minimising hazards and safety risks in the environment' (ACECQA 2011b: 51).

Regulations relating to outdoor space requirements are another factor that potentially limits outdoor play provision. Under the National Regulations, the minimum outdoor space allocation is 7 m^2 per child. A recent survey of 225 centres from across Australia indicated that 39 per cent of centres had the minimum 7 m^2 per child while 58 per cent of centres exceeded this requirement and the remainder had less than the minimum required space (Little 2013). As a general guide, Mauffette et al. (1999, cited by Herrington and Lesmeister 2006) recommend 13.5 m^2 as necessary for the provision of diverse outdoor experiences that meet safety standards. Other studies have examined outdoor space by m^2 and number of children on an average day. For example, a recent study conducted in Brisbane centres found mean typical daily attendance to be 60 (range 20–113) and mean outdoor space to be 413 m^2 (range 200–672) (Sugiyama et al. 2012). These researchers also noted that there is a need for empirical evidence on the minimum size of an outdoor play area below which physical activity is compromised. By comparison, Norwegian centres typically have outdoor areas much greater than this (see Sandseter, Chapter 8, this

Table 10.2 National regulations and NQS quality areas and standards relevant to outdoor play provision

Quality area	Standards	National regulation
1 Educational program and practice	1.1 An approved learning framework informs the development of a curriculum that enhances each child's learning and development 1.1.6 Each child's agency is promoted, enabling them to make choices and decisions and influence events and their world 1.2 Educators and co-ordinators are focused, active and reflective in designing and delivering the program for each child	4.1 Educational program and practice 73 (2) An educational program is to contribute to the following outcomes for each child: (a) the child will have a strong sense of identity; (b) the child will be connected with and contribute to his or her world; (c) the child will have a strong sense of wellbeing; (d) the child will be a confident and involved learner; (e) the child will be an effective communicator
2 Children's health and safety	2.2 Healthy eating and physical activity are embedded in the program for children 2.2.2 Physical activity is promoted through planned and spontaneous experiences and is appropriate for each child 2.3 Each child is protected 2.3.1 Children are adequately supervised at all times 2.3.2 Every reasonable precaution is taken to protect children from harm and any hazard likely to cause injury	4.2 Children's health and safety 85 Incident, injury, trauma and illness policies and procedures The incident, injury, trauma and illness policies and procedures of an education and care service required under regulation 168 must include procedures to be followed by nominated supervisors and staff members of, and volunteers at, the service in the event that a child: (a) is injured; or (b) becomes ill; or (c) suffers a trauma 86 Notification to parents of incident, injury, trauma and illness

3 Physical environment

3.1 The design and location of the premises is appropriate for the operation of a service

3.1.1 Outdoor and indoor spaces, buildings, furniture, equipment, facilities and resources are suitable for their purpose

3.1.3 Facilities are designed or adapted to ensure access and participation by every child in the service and to allow flexible use, and interaction between indoor and outdoor space

3.2 The environment is inclusive, promotes competence, independent exploration and learning through play

3.2.1 Outdoor and indoor spaces are designed and organised to engage every child in quality experiences in both built and natural environments

3.2.2 Resources, materials and equipment are sufficient in number, organised in ways that ensure appropriate and effective implementation of the program and allow for multiple uses

3.3 The service takes an active role in caring for its environment and contributes to a sustainable future

3.3.2 Children are supported to become environmentally responsible and show respect for the environment

4.3 Physical environment

108 Space requirements: outdoor space

(2) The approved provider of an education and care service must ensure that, for each child being educated and cared for by the service, the education and care service premises has at least 7 square metres of unencumbered outdoor space

113 Outdoor space: natural environment

The approved provider of a centre-based service must ensure that the outdoor spaces provided at the education and care service premises allow children to explore and experience the natural environment

114 Outdoor space: shade

The approved provider of a centre-based service must ensure that outdoor spaces provided at the education and care service premises include adequate shaded areas to protect children from overexposure to ultraviolet radiation from the sun

(Continued)

Table 10.2 National regulations and NQS quality areas and standards relevant to outdoor play provision (*continued*)

Quality area	Standards	National regulation
4 Staffing arrangements	4.1 Staffing arrangements enhance children's learning and development and ensure their safety and wellbeing	115 Premises designed to facilitate supervision The approved provider of a centre-based service must ensure that the education and care service premises (including toilets and nappy change facilities) are designed and maintained in a way that facilitates supervision of children at all times that they are being educated and cared for by the service, having regard to the need to maintain the rights and dignity of the children
5 Relationships with children	5.1 Respectful and equitable relationships are developed and maintained with each child 5.1.2 Every child is able to engage with educators in meaningful, open interactions that support the acquisition of skills for life and learning 5.1.3 Each child is supported to feel secure, confident and included. 5.2 Each child is supported to build and maintain sensitive relationships with other children and adults 5.2.1 Every child is supported to work with, learn from and help others through collaborative learning opportunities	4.5 Relationships with children 155 Interactions with children An approved provider must take reasonable steps to ensure that the education and care service provides education and care to children in a way that: (b) allows the children to undertake experiences that develop self-reliance and self-esteem

Sources: ACECQA (2011b); Ministerial Council for Education, Early Childhood Development and Youth Affairs (2011).

volume). Moser and Martinsen (2010) found that the kindergartens in their study had large outdoor spaces, averaging 2600 m^2 or approximately 47 m^2 per child. Access to these large outdoor areas provided children with rich and varied outdoor experiences that fostered engagement with nature as well as providing 'secret' places where individual children or small groups of two or three children could withdraw from the general 'hustle and bustle' of the kindergarten and experience relative peace and quiet. Moser and Martinsen suggest that this is important for children's mental health and wellbeing. In comparison, the considerably smaller outdoor space allocation in Australian EC centres limits the potential for such experiences.

Lack of space has also been identified as restricting the diversity and complexity of physical play especially the provision of equipment such as swings or climbing apparatus due to requirements under the Australian Standards for playground equipment. When only minimum space requirements are met, few centres have sufficiently large outdoor areas to accommodate challenging activities that incorporate a range of heights and complexity while still maintaining the required fall zones (Little 2010). Unfortunately, these restrictions contribute to a lack of physical activity in young Australian children. For example, two recent studies have found between 46 per cent (Dyment and Coleman 2012) and 66 per cent (Sugiyama et al. 2012) of centre-based playtime outdoors involved sedentary behaviours.

These findings are even more troubling when considered in the context of children's daily lives and opportunities for outdoor play. A recent Sydney study, for example, found 84 per cent of children were driven to childcare and a further 7 per cent were sometimes driven and sometimes walked (Partridge 2007). Only 8 per cent usually walked to childcare. Thus it seems that on the days of attendance at childcare, the options for children to engage in active play and even meet the minimum requirements for daily physical activity, are extremely limited. Recent evidence indicates that on weekdays, over 40 per cent of Australian pre-schoolers do not meet daily physical activity requirements based on National Association for Sport and Physical Education guidelines (Okely et al. 2009).

In contrast, opportunities for outdoor play in schools is limited to periods of free play during recess and lunch, and more structured play or physical activity provided as part of the PDHPE curriculum. A recent study of Sydney schools found an average of 4.8 m^2 of outdoor playspace per child (Engelen et al. 2013). Data from the same study found much of children's outdoor time was spent in eating-related behaviours that either prevented or compromised full engagement in physical and social play (Wyver et al. 2012). The restriction of opportunities for active play becomes more disturbing when seen in the context of the typical weekday. Seventy one per cent of 4- to 9-year-olds usually travel to school by car. The major barriers to walking or cycling are parental concerns about children being assaulted/molested and concerns they will take risks when walking with other children (Salmon et al. 2007).

Opportunities for risk-taking in centres and schools

The nature of outdoor play and outdoor environments, especially natural playspaces, offers vast potential for diverse experiences. The opportunities for open-ended and spontaneous exploration and discovery that the outdoor environment offers, means that outcomes can at times be unpredictable. This unpredictability is a core aspect of risk-taking. Risk-taking can be defined as behaviours that result in outcomes that are uncertain but are an integral part of learning and development as children test the limits of their ability and move out of their comfort zone to engage in new experiences and acquire new skills; however, as the discussion in the previous section suggests, the need to balance support for children's engagement in challenging, risky play with the requirement for accountability means that opportunities for risk-taking may be restricted. In a previous publication (see Little and Wyver 2008), we proposed that there were a number of potential factors that lead to risk minimization in outdoor play. These included high child:staff ratios, external regulations, an inadequate understanding of the benefits of risk-taking, and poor outdoor environments. These factors impact on the quality of outdoor play which then potentially leads to a range of negative short- and long-term outcomes. In this section, we examine opportunities for risk-taking in centres and schools.

With the introduction of the Early Years Learning Framework there has come a focus on risk-taking as an integral part of children's learning and development as the following excepts illustrate. 'Children develop their emerging autonomy, inter-dependence, resilience and sense of agency when they take considered risks in their decision-making and cope with the unexpected' (DEEWR 2009: 22). 'Children become strong in their social and emotional wellbeing when they make choices, accept challenges, take considered risks, manage change and cope with frustrations and the unexpected' (DEEWR 2009: 31). When educators 'plan learning environments with appropriate levels of challenge where children are encouraged to explore, experiment and take appropriate risks in their learning' (DEEWR 2009: 35) children become confident and involved learners. This statement acknowledges the important role of the EC educator in providing learning environments that support challenge and risk-taking. When teachers use their knowledge of individual children to identify and understand individual differences in children's patterns of risk-taking, they are able to tailor experiences that support children's engagement with challenge and risk within their own comfort zone. For example, teachers can provide smaller, incremental challenges and lots of support for the child who is wary about taking risks and avoids situations that take them out of their comfort zone. At the other end of the spectrum, children who are predisposed to taking high levels of risk are provided with sufficiently challenging and stimulating activities so that they do not engage in inappropriate risk-taking that involves a high risk of injury.

However, as the discussion of the regulatory environment in the previous section suggests, teachers often experience tension in balancing their desire to provide challenging activities that allow children to experience and learn from taking calculated risks, and complying with regulatory requirements. A further two issues, training and ratios, are also thought to have an impact on opportunities for risky play. Although minimum requirements for each are specified within national regulations, some issues sit outside the regulatory environment.

Training

The level of staff training in Australian EC settings has a positive association with children's physical activity, possibly due to increased understanding of physical activity and development (e.g. Sugiyama et al. 2012). Yet Australian EC teachers feel unprepared for physically active experiences with children (Coleman and Dyment 2013). Unlike Norwegian EC teachers, Australian teachers generally work from theoretical bases that emphasize the higher order cognitive-linguistic aspects of development rather than theories that emphasize direct connection with the physical environment and this may make it more difficult to translate beliefs about physical activity into practice (Sandseter et al. 2012). Additional constraints for Australian teachers include the need to defer to the advice provided by regulatory authority assessors who, in the absence of knowledge of individual children's abilities can only base their judgment on the physical environment. Consequently, decisions made by assessors are likely to be different to those of the teachers.

Ratios and supervision

One way of ensuring that children's safety is promoted in the outdoor environment is through supervision. The NQS state that, in planning for children's learning experiences, educators need to 'ensure that all areas used by children are effectively supervised, including when children are participating in high-risk activities' (ACECQA 2011b: 72).

By providing the appropriate level of supervision that is neither overly directive nor overly protective, EC teachers 'ensure children are alerted to safety issues and encouraged to develop the skills to assess and minimize risks to their own safety' (ACECQA 2011b: 72). Higher staff:child ratios have been associated with higher levels of preschoolers' physical activity (Sugiyama et al. 2012). Staff report difficulties in facilitating active play when ratios are less than optimal (Coleman and Dyment 2013). National standards for children from 36 months to school age are between 1:10 to 1:11 and may contribute to staff taking conservative options for physically active and risky play.

An observational study of 4- and 5-year-old children's outdoor play in six preschools in Sydney revealed that the outdoor play experiences provided for children mainly involved activities that were very low risk and presented little or no challenge for the children (see Little et al. 2011). They provided limited opportunities for children to experience risky play activities such as those described by Sandseter (2007) especially those involving height, speed, play with tools and rough and tumble play.

Conclusion

Despite Australia's commitment to high quality education and care, limitations continue in opportunities for children to engage in a full range of challenging play and learning experiences. We believe these limitations can be overcome, to some extent, by shifting from centralized regulatory decisions about children's environments and emphasizing the importance of localized and individualized decisions made by qualified staff. We also believe greater responsibility for decision-making by teachers will lead to children engaging in a broader range of experiences with their natural environment and enhancing their connection with the unique ecology of Australia.

References

ABS (Australian Bureau of Statistics) (2010) 1370.0 – Measures of Australia's Progress: Population distribution. http://www.abs.gov.au/ausstats/abs@.nsf/Lookup/by%20Subject/1370.0~2010~Chapter~Population%20distribution%20%283.3%29 (accessed 6 January 2014).

ACECQA (Australian Children's Education and Care Quality Authority) (2011a) *Guide to the National Quality Framework.* http://acecqa.gov.au/links-and-resources/national-quality-framework-resources/ (accessed 6 January 2014).

ACECQA (Australian Children's Education and Care Quality Authority) (2011b) *Guide to the National Quality Standard.* http://acecqa.gov.au/national-quality-framework/national-quality-standard/ (accessed 6 January 2014).

Bown, K. and Sumsion, J. (2007) Voices from the other side of the fence: early childhood teachers' experiences with mandatory regulatory requirements, *Contemporary Issues in Early Childhood*, 8(1): 30–49.

Brennan, D. (2007) The ABC of child care politics. *Australian Journal of Social Issues*, 42(2): 213–25.

Coleman, B. and Dyment, J.E. (2013) Factors that limit and enable preschool-aged children's physical activity on child care centre playgrounds. *Journal of Early Childhood Research*, 11(3): 203–21.

DEEWR (Australian Government Department of Education, Employment, and Workplace Relations) (2009) *Belonging, Being and Becoming. The Early Years Learning Framework for Australia.* Canberra: DEEWR.

Dollman, J., Norton, K. and Norton, L. (2005) Evidence for secular trends in children's physical activity behaviour, *British Journal of Sports Medicine*, 39(12): 892–7.

Drabsch, T. (2013) *The Australian Curriculum Briefing Paper No 1/2013*. http://www.parliament.nsw.gov.au/prod/parlment/publications.nsf/0/B18363C26 EC0F93ACA257B1800144FDE/$File/The%20Australian%20Curriculum.pdf (accessed 5 April 2013).

Dyment, J.E. and Coleman, B. (2012) The intersection of physical activity opportunities and the role of early childhood educators during outdoor play: perceptions and reality, *Australasian Journal of Early Childhood*, 37(1): 90–8.

Engelen, L., Bundy, A.C., Naughton, G. et al. (2013) Increasing physical activity in young primary school children – it's child's play: a cluster randomised controlled trial, *Preventive Medicine*, 56(5): 319–25.

Fenech, M., Sumsion, J., and Goodfellow, J. (2006) The regulatory environment in long day care: a 'double-edged sword' for early childhood professional practice, *Australian Journal of Early Childhood*, 31(3): 49–58.

Flannery, T. (1994) *The Future Eaters: An Ecological History of the Australasian Lands and People*. New York: Grove Press.

Herrington, S., and Lesmeister, C. (2006) The design of landscapes at child-care centres: Seven Cs, *Landscape Research*, 31(1): 63–82.

Hosking, S. (2011) The aspirational citizen and neo-liberal hegemony: a discourse theory analysis. Unpublished doctoral dissertation. University of NSW.

Howard, S. and Gill, J. (2001) 'It's like we're a normal way and everyone else is different': Australian children's constructions of citizenship and national identity. *Educational Studies*, 27(1): 87–103.

Lee, B. (2011) *Australia Days: Bogue nation: Walking with bogans*. Centre for Contemporary Photography, Victoria Arts. http://www.brendanlee.com/site. php?n=Main.BogueNationWalkingWithBogans (accessed 28 March 2013).

Little, H. (2010) Risk, challenge and safety in outdoor play: pedagogical and regulatory tensions, *Asia-Pacific Journal of Research in Early Childhood Education*, 4(1): 3–24.

Little, H. (2013) Outdoor environments and play provision in Australia: promoting risk-taking and physically challenging play in early childhood settings. Paper presented at the 23rd EECERA Conference, Tallinn, Estonia.

Little, H. and Wyver, S. (2008) Outdoor play: does avoiding the risks reduce the benefits? *Australian Journal of Early Childhood*, 33(2): 33–40.

Little, H., Wyver, S. and Gibson, F. (2011) The influence of play context and adult attitudes on young children's physical risk-taking during outdoor play, *European Early Childhood Education Research Journal*, 19(1): 113–31.

Ministerial Council for Education, Early Childhood Development and Youth Affairs (2011) *Education and Care Services National Regulations*. http://www.legislation.nsw.gov.au/sessionalview/sessional/subordleg/2011-653.pdf (accessed 6 January 2014).

Moser, T. and Martinsen, M. (2010) The outdoor environment in Norwegian kindergartens as pedagogical space for toddlers' play, learning and development, *European Early Childhood Education Research Journal*, 18(4): 457–71.

Okely, A.D., Trost, S.G., Steele, J.R., Cliff, D.P. and Mickle, K. (2009) Adherence to physical activity and electronic media guidelines in Australian pre-school children, *Journal of Paediatrics and Child Health*, 45: 5–8.

Partridge, E. (2007) *Active Transport for Childcare Centres: A Case Study and Resource for Councils*. SSROC.

Productivity Commission (2011) *Early Child Development Workforce: Productivity Commission Draft Research Report*. Canberra: Commonwealth of Australia.

Salmon, J., Salmon, L., Crawford, D.A., Hume, C. and Timperio, A. (2007) Associations among individual, social, and environmental barriers and children's walking or cycling to school, *American Journal of Health Promotion*, 22(2): 107–13.

Sandseter, E.B. (2007) Categorising risky play – how can we identify risk-taking in children's play? *European Early Childhood Education Research Journal*, 15(2): 237–52.

Sandseter, E.B.H., Little, H. and Wyver, S. (2012) Do theory and pedagogy have an impact on provisions for outdoor learning? A comparison of approaches in Australia and Norway, *Journal of Adventure Education and Outdoor Learning*, 12(3): 167–82.

Sugiyama, T., Okely, A.D., Master, J.M. and Moore, G.T. (2012) Attributes of child care centres and outdoor play areas associated with preschoolers' physical activity and sedentary behavior, *Environment and Behavior*, 44(3): 334–49.

Trading Economics (2013) Urban population in Australia. http://www.tradingeconomics.com/australia/urban-population-wb-data.html (accessed 6 January 2014).

Waniganayake, M., Cheeseman, S., Fenech, M., Hadley, F. and Shepherd, W. (2012) *Leadership: Contexts and Complexities in Early Childhood Education*. Melbourne: Oxford University Press.

Wyver, S., Engelen, L., Bundy, A. and Naughton, G. (2012) What's eating into school recess? Implications of extended eating for free play and physical activity, in J. Wright (ed.) *Proceedings of the Australian Association for Research in Education Conference*. Sydney: University of Sydney. http://www1.aare.edu.au/pages/static/conference.aspx?y=2012&s=1050&so=&f (accessed 6 January 2014).

Wyver, S., Tranter, P., Naughton, G. et al. (2010) Ten ways to restrict children's freedom to play: the problem of surplus safety, *Contemporary Issues in Early Childhood*, 11(3): 263–77.

Index

Locators shown in *italics* refer to figures and tables.